T0133399

Departement of Informatics
University of Fribourg (Switzerland)

Towards a Secure and User Friendly Authentication Method for Public Wireless Networks

THESIS

presented to the Faculty of Science of the University of Fribourg (Switzerland)
in consideration for the award of the academic grade of
Doctor scientiarum informaticarum

by

CAROLIN LATZE

from

Germany

Thesis No: 1675
UniPrint, Fribourg
2010

Bibliografische Information der Deutschen Nationalbibliothek

Die Deutsche Nationalbibliothek verzeichnet diese Publikation in der
Deutschen Nationalbibliografie; detaillierte bibliografische Daten sind
im Internet über http://dnb.d-nb.de abrufbar.

ISBN 978-3-8325-2694-8

Logos Verlag Berlin GmbH
Comeniushof, Gubener Str. 47,
10243 Berlin
Tel.: +49 (0)30 42 85 10 90
Fax: +49 (0)30 42 85 10 92
INTERNET: http://www.logos-verlag.de

Acknowledgments

First of all I want to thank Prof. Dr. U. Ultes-Nitsche, head of the Telecommunications, Networks, and Security research group (TNS) at the University of Fribourg for supervising my work. Furthermore, I want to thank my colleagues in the research group, namely Thierry Nicola, Christoph Ehret, Michael Hayoz, Stephan Krenn, Stefania Barzan, Joel Allred, Reto König, Oliver Spycher and Ronny Standtke for their comments and discussions. I also thank my master students Andreas Ruppen and Marc Käser.

I also want to thank the experts Prof. Dr. Torsten Braun and Prof. Dr. Rüdiger Grimm for their comments and feedback.

Since this thesis was a rather practical work I am very thankful for the discussions and support of Dr. Stefan Mangold, Martin Lenze, Ernst von Bühren, and Josua Hiller at Swisscom NIT. They helped me a lot in evaluating my ideas against real world constraints. Furthermore, since I was employed at Swisscom ICC during the last two years of my thesis, I want to thank my colleagues there for their support and consideration of the time I needed for my thesis, namely Ramun Berger, Dr. Andreas Jarosch, and Dr. Thomas Zasowski.

Lastly but most importantly I want to thank my family and my partner Florian for their support during my university years.

Abstract

The goal of this thesis was to develop a secure and user friendly authentication scheme for public wireless networks (PWLANs). In contrast to private wireless networks, public wireless networks need a proper authentication scheme for several reasons. First of all, the network operator must be able to identify a user in case an incident happens. Furthermore, such networks are usually controlled by a commercial operator who will hardly allow access for free. This leads to the need for a secure and reliable authentication method. However, the authentication method must be user-friendly too in order to be acceptable. The only "wireless networks" users know so far are cellular networks, which are very easy to use. Users do therefore ask for a comparable experience in public wireless networks. This is obviously not given for the captive portals that are the most common authentication method today. Captive portals use the webbrowser as an authentication device by blocking all traffic until the first HTTP request is sent. That message redirects the user to the captive portal page where she is asked to give her user credentials. This is obviously rather complicated since the user has to open the browser in any case. Furthermore, captive portals usually carry a lot of advertisements which makes it impossible to automate the login process.

In order to overcome the security and usability problems of captive portals, operators provide EAP-SIM authentication. EAP-SIM uses the SIM credentials for PWLAN authentication. Since people are used to SIM cards due to the cellular networks, the acceptance for this authentication method is high. Furthermore, EAP-SIM provides a good level of security since the user credentials are held within trusted hardware. However, most of the devices used in public wireless networks do not have a SIM slot out of the box which renders EAP-SIM again uncomfortable.

Since the idea to store user credentials in trusted hardware is appealing, this thesis evaluates the Trusted Platform Module (TPM) as an authentication device. The TPM is a small cryptographic module built into almost every new computer. This thesis shows how to use the TPM as an authentication device in EAP-TLS. Furthermore, this thesis shows theoretical and real world evaluations of EAP-TLS with the TPM. It will be shown that this authentication method provides a good level of security as well as good usability.

Zusammenfassung

Das Ziel dieser Arbeit war es, eine sichere und benutzerfreundliche Authentifizierungsmethode für öffentliche Funknetzwerke zu entwickeln. Im Gegensatz zu privaten Funknetzwerken ist eine sichere Authentifizerung in öffentlichen Netzen aus verschiedensten Gründen zwingend notwendig. Zunächst einmal muss der Netzwerkanbieter in der Lage sein, Benutzer im Falle eines Vorfalles eindeutig zu identifizieren. Des weiteren werden öffentliche Funknetzwerke häufig von kommerziellen Netzanbietern zur Verfügung gestellt, die damit Geld verdienen wollen und müssen. All dies verlangt nach einer sicheren und zuverlässigen Authentifizierungsmethode. Damit eine Authentifizierungsmethode wirklich akzeptabel ist, muss sie jedoch auch benutzerfreundlich sein. Die einzigen Funknetzwerke, die Benutzern heutzutage geläufig sind, sind Zelluläre Netze. Da diese Netzwerke für die Nutzer sehr einfach zu bedienen sind, wollen sie ein ähnliches Erlebnis in öffentlichen Funknetzwerken haben. Dies ist nicht gegeben bei sogenannten Captive Portals, welche heutzutage die meist gebrauchte Authentifizierungsmethode in öffentlichen Funknetzwerken sind. Captive Portals verwenden den Webbrowser als Authentifizierungsmodul indem sie jeglichen Datenverkehr blockieren bis die erste HTTP Anfrage gesendet wurde. Diese Anfrage leitet den Benutzer dann auf das Captive Portal um, wo er seine Benutzerdaten eingeben muss. Dies ist offensichtlich sehr kompliziert, da der Benutzer in jedem Fall einen Webbrowser öffnen muss. Des weiteren zeigen Captive Portals häufig sehr viel Werbung, weswegen ein automaisches Login unmöglich ist.

Um die Sicherheitsprobleme und die fehlende Benutzerfreundlichkeit von Captive Portals zu umgehen, bieten Netzwerkanbieter die EAP-SIM Authentifizierung an. EAP-SIM verwendet die Benutzerdaten der SIM Karte zur Authentifizierung in öffentlichen Funknetzwerken. Da die Benutzer aus Zellulären Netzen an SIM Karten gewöhnt sind, ist die Akzeptanz bei dieser Authentifizierungsmethode sehr gross. Des weiteren bietet EAP-SIM ein gutes Mass an Sicherheit, da die Benutzerdaten in einem vetrauenswürdigen Hardwaremodul abgelegt sind. Da aber die meisten Geräte, welche in öffentlichen Funknetzwerken verwendet werden, keinen SIM Steckplatz haben, ist EAP-SIM ebenfalls eine unkomfortable Authentifizierungsmethode.

Da die Idee, Benutzerdaten in vertrauenswürdiger Hardware zu speichern, sehr verlockend ist, wurde in dieser Arbeit das Trusted Platform Module (TPM) als Authentifizierungsmodul evaluiert. Das TPM ist ein kleines kryptographisches Modul, welches heutzutage in nahezu jeden neuen Computer eingebaut wird. Diese Arbeit zeigt auf, wie man das TPM als Authentifizierungsmodule in EAP-TLS verwenden kann. Des weiteren evaluiert diese Arbeit die theoretische und praktische Anwendbarkeit von EAP-TLS mit dem TPM. Es wird gezeigt, dass diese Authentifizierungsmethode ein sehr gutes Mass an Sicherheit und eine gute Benutzerfreundlichkeit aufweist.

Contents

List of Figures

Listings

1
Introduction

The world today is an always-on world. Almost all applications are expected to be usable anywhere and at any time. For instance, users want to update their Facebook profile wherever they are, read e-mails, or share pictures of the moment. The only network available so far is the cellular network. The second generation of cellular networks, the so called GSM network, already allows for data traffic, but only with limited speed, and it is rather expensive. The third generation cellular network called UMTS allows for higher bandwidths, but a theoretical maximum of 2 Mb/s is still very limited. During the past years, more and more wireless computer networks have emerged that provide higher bandwidths and are perceived as being inexpensive. Soon there was the desire to make these networks available everywhere and for everybody. The first attempts to open wireless networks have been made by private persons who opened their private wireless networks for everybody passing by in front of their house. Soon after, the first companies like FON (FON, 2009) tried to organize and professionalize these open private wireless networks. However, without an operator-controlled and organized infrastructure, such networks will always be limited to single clusters, for instance in big cities. Nowadays the big operators start deploying large organized so called public wireless networks. With the broader propagation of these PWLANs, users expect a cellular network-like experience in such networks. That means they must be easy to use. However, as in cellular networks, operator-controlled PWLANs need an authentication, authorization, and accounting infrastructure for chargeability and incident tracking. In contrast to cellular networks, wireless networks did not specify those features right from the beginning. This thesis concentrates on the authentication aspects, where cellular networks have a huge advantage. They defined a secure module holding the user's identity right from the beginning. That module called SIM is integrated into every device built for cellular networks (or at least there is a slot to carry the SIM). Such a module was completely missing in public wireless networks. It was comparable to a small revolution when in 2001, the TCG released the first specification for the Trusted Platform Module (TPM). A TPM is a secure module built into almost every new computer that provides storage for cryptographic keys as well as some cryptographic functionality like RSA encryption and random number generation. This work shows how to use the TPM in an authentication protocol for public wireless networks.

1.1 Structure of this Thesis

The thesis is organized as follows: Chapter 2 discusses the details of second and third generation cellular networks. It starts with an architectural overview, discusses the networks' security features as well as the authentication protocols. In short, Chapter 2 discusses the network that provides the user experience that is desired for public wireless networks, too.

Chapter 3 deals with the technical basis of wireless networks. This includes the architecture as well as the authentication framework and the new device identifier standard which already mentions the TPM.

The authentication protocols used in public wireless networks today are presented in Chapter 4. Those protocols include the simplest "protocol" that realizes user authentication using captive portals as well as the Extensible Authentication Protocol (EAP) methods EAP-SIM, EAP-AKA, and EAP-TLS.

Having thus discussed the basics of public wireless networks and their authentication protocols, Chapter 5 explains the background and specification of Trusted Platform Modules (TPMs). Furthermore, Chapter 5 shows how to write programs that make use of a TPM and presents two possible applications of the TPM.

Finally, Chapter 6 presents a TLS extension for TPMs that allows to use TPMs in EAP-TLS to authenticate users in public wireless networks. Furthermore, Chapter 6 discusses a zero-configuration protocol that allows users to connect to EAP-TLS secured networks without any prerequisites in case the TLS TPM extension is used.

A discussion of a proof of concept prototype showing the usage of TPMs in EAP-TLS as well as the zero-configuration protocol is given in Chapter 7. That chapter shows how easy and transparent the implementations are.

The last chapter, Chapter 8, presents some performance measurements and feasibility studies of EAP-TLS with support of the TPM. Additionally, the zero-configuration protocol has been evaluated against real world constraints. Last, an outlook on how to make use of those protocols in a commercial environment is given.

It has to be mentioned that especially Chapters 2 to 5 are based on well known standards. In order to remain consistent with the standards, this thesis uses the terminology used in the official standard documents. However, this may lead to inconsistency between the different chapters. In order to make the chapters as readable as possible, they start with a short explanation of the terminology used.

1.2 Pre-Publications

During the work on this topic, several papers and two Internet Drafts have been published:

KiVS 2007 C. Latze, U. Ultes-Nitsche: Using a Trusted Platform Module to enable a Secure Usage of Nodes in Company Networks (An extension of the AEGIS approach), 15. ITG/GI - Fachtagung (KIVS 2007), Bern, Switzerland, February 2007

SoftCOM 2007 C.Latze, U.Ultes-Nische, F.Baumgartner: Strong Mutual Authentication in a User-Friendly Way in EAP-TLS, 15th International Conference on Software, Telecommunications and Computer Networks (SoftCOM 2007), Split - Dubrovnik, Croatia, September 2007

CSNA 2007 C.Latze, U.Ultes-Nitsche: Stronger Authentication in e-commerce. How to protect even naive users against phishing, pharming, and MITM attacks, Communication Systems, Networks, and Applications (CSNA 2007), Beijing, China, October 2007

ISSA 2008 C.Latze, U.Ultes-Nitsche: A Proof-of-Concept Implementation of EAP-TLS with TPM support, Innovative Minds (ISSA 2008), Johannesburg, South Africa, July 2008

SoftCOM 2008 C.Latze, U.Ultes-Nitsche: Roaming, Accounting and Seamless Handover in EAP-TLS Authenticated Networks, 16th International Conference on Software, Telecommunications and Computer Networks (SoftCOM 2008), Split - Dubrovnik, Croatia, September 2008

LCN 2008 C.Latze, U.Ultes-Nitsche, F.Baumgartner: Towards a Zero Configuration Authentication Scheme for 802.11 Based Networks, IEEE Conference on Local Computer Networks (LCN 2008), Montreal, Canada, October 2008

ISSA 2009 C.Latze, A.Ruppen, U.Ultes-Nitsche: A Proof of Concept Implementation of A Secure E-Commerce Authentication Scheme, Information Security South Africa (ISSA 2009), Johannesburg, South Africa, July 2009

LCN 2009 C.Latze, U.Ultes-Nitsche, J.Hiller: EAP-TPM: A New Authentication Protocol for IEEE 802.11 Based Networks, Demo at the IEEE Conference on Local Computer Networks (LCN 2009), Zurich, Switzerland, October 2009

Furthermore, the work has been presented in three technical reports and discussed in two presentations:

RVS Retreat 2007 Torsten Braun, Ulrich Ultes-Nitsche, Marc Brogle, Dragan Milic, Patrick Lauer, Thomas Staub, Gerald Wagenknecht, Markus Anwander, Markus Waelchli, Markus Wulff, Carolin Latze, Michael Hayoz, Christoph Ehret, Thierry Nicola: RVS Retreat 2007, Quarten, Switzerland, June 2007

BeNeFri Summerschool 2008 Marc Brogle, Dragan Milic, Markus Anwander, Gerald Wagenknecht, Markus Waelchli, Torsten Braun, Raphael Kummer, Markus Wulff, Ronny Standtke, Heiko Sturzrehm, Etienne Riviere, Pascal Felber, Stephan Krenn, Christoph Ehret, Carolin Latze, Philipp Hurni, Thomas Staub: BeNeFri Summer School 2008 on Dependable Systems, Quarten, Switzerland, June 2008

BeNeFri Summerschool 2009 Marc Brogle, Sabina Serbu, Dragan Milic, Markus Anwander, Philipp Hurni, Christian Spielvogel, Claire Fautsch, Derin Harmanci, Lukas Charles, Heiko Sturzrehm, Gerald Wagenknecht, Torsten

Braun, Thomas Staub, Carolin Latze, Ronny Standke: BeNeFri Summer School 2009 on Dependable Systems, Mnchenwiler, Switzerland, June 2009

ITG Fachgruppe 5.2.2 2009 EAP-TPM: A New Authentication Method for 802.11 Based Networks, ITG Fachgruppe 5.2.2, Fachgruppentreffen 18.06.2009, Heidelberg, Germany

ITValley 2009 EAP-TPM: A New Authentication Method for Public Wireless Networks, ITValley Fribourg, 28.09.2009, Fribourg, Switzerland

Last, there are two Internet Drafts resulting out of this work with the second being the one to be pushed onward.

EAP-TPM Internet Draft: Extensible Authentication Protocol Method for Trusted Computing Groups (TCG) Trusted Platform Module

TLS-TPM-extns Internet Draft: Transport Layer Security (TLS) Extensions for the Trusted Platform Module (TPM)

2

Second and Third Generation Cellular Networks

As it was one of the goals to develop an authentication scheme for wireless LANs that makes them as comfortable to use as GSM or UMTS networks, it is worth having a look at the architecture and authentication methods of GSM/ UMTS networks. This chapter starts with an overview of the GSM architecture and authentication, goes on with the UMTS architecture and authentication and ends with a conclusion.

─────────────── **Notations** ───────────────

The terms and abbreviations used in this chapter follow the GSM 01.02 document (ETSI, 2001) and ETSI TR 121 905 (ETSI, 2009a).

The vocabulary in GSM does slightly differ from the vocabulary used in UMTS: **mobile stations** in GSM are called **user equipment** in UMTS.

2.1 Second Generation Cellular Networks

The Global System for Mobile Communication (GSM) was introduced into the consumer market only in 1991 after almost 10 years of standardization work. In 1982, the European Conference of Postal and Telecommunications Administrations (CEPT - Conférence Européenne des Administrations des Postes et des Telecommunications) founded a group called Groupe Spécial Mobile - abbreviated GSM - to work on a unified mobile communications standard for Europe. It was in 1991 that the group was renamed into Standard Mobile Group (SMG) and GSM became the new name for the standard called "Global System for Mobile Communication" as mentioned above.

This section starts with an introduction into the GSM network architecture, outlines some security considerations and concludes with some details about GSM authentication and encryption.

2.1.1 Architecture

GSM is a standard for voice and non-voice services and facilities in mobile networks accessible for any mobile subscriber in at least any country of the CEPT.

The GSM network architecture is specified in (ETSI, 2001) and illustrated in Figure 2.1.

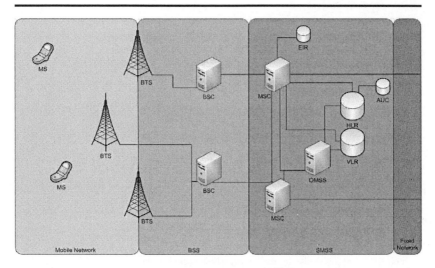

Figure 2.1: GSM Network Overview. MS = Mobile Stations, BSS = Base Station System, BTS = Base Transceiver Station, BSC = Base Station Controller, SMSS = Switching and Management Subsystem, MSC = Mobile Switching Center, HLR = Home Location Register, VLR = Visitor Location Register, OMSS = Operation and Maintenance Subsystem, EIR = Equipment Identity Register, AUC = Authentication Center.

The *Mobile Stations (MS)* associate themselves with so called *Base Transceiver Stations (BTS)* via radio. The BTS is connected to a *Base Station Controller (BSC)* who surveys the connections and triggers cell handovers if needed. One BSC usually controls several 10 or 100 BTS.

BTS and BSC together form the *Base Station System (BSS)* which is responsible for the traffic and signaling channels. The access method for those channels is Time Division Multiple Access (TDMA) (ETSI, 2002).

The BSS is followed by the *Switching and Management Subsystem (SMSS)* starting with the *Mobile Switching Center (MSC)*. The MSC is the interface between the mobile network technologies and the fixed telephone system. Furthermore it is responsible for the general call handling, the handover procedure, the management of radio resources and the exchange of signaling information with other MSCs. The MSC has connections to the *Home Location Register (HLR)*, the *Visitor Location*

Register (VLR) and the optional *Equipment Identity Registry (EIR)*. The HLR holds subscriber information like the *International Mobile Subscriber Number (IMSI)*, the mobile station's ISDN number and its current VLR address in case of roaming. The latter is needed to route incoming calls correctly and is called *Mobile Subscriber Roaming Number (MSRN)*. The VLR stores subscriber information like the IMSI and the exact location of a roaming subscriber in its area. The EIR stores the serial numbers of the mobile devices used in the network. The HLR is connected to the *Authentication Center (AUC)* which is responsible for the authentication of mobile stations. The authentication algorithm(s) specified and used right from the beginning of GSM are explained in Section 2.1.3.

Last but not least, a GSM network needs an *Operation and Management Subsystem (OMSS)* that monitors and controls the network control functions and the MSCs, BSCs and BTSs.

2.1.2 Security Considerations

The security features provided by a GSM network are specified in (ETSI, 2006). There are five mandatory security features:

1. International Mobile Subscriber Identity (IMSI) confidentiality

2. IMSI authentication

3. user data confidentiality on physical connections

4. connection-less user data confidentiality,

5. signaling information element confidentiality

IMSI confidentiality means that the IMSI must never be disclosed to unauthorized entities. This is usually ensured by storing the IMSI inside a trusted module called Subscriber Identity Module (SIM). Furthermore, the IMSI is usually only used for the first authentication. Afterwards the subscriber gets a temporary IMSI used for the rest of the session. IMSI confidentiality is required since an IMSI as specified in (ETSI, 1993b) tells a lot about the subscriber. It includes his Mobile Country Code (MCC), the Mobile Network Code (MNC), and the Mobile Subscriber Identification Number (MSIN).

IMSI authentication is required to avoid unauthorized network usage. It is triggered by the network if the subscriber applies for a server. For details about GSM authentication see Section 2.1.3.

User data confidentiality on physical connections aims at ensuring the privacy of subscriber information on traffic channels using encryption algorithms described in Section 2.1.3.

Connection-less user data confidentiality works analogously to the aforementioned feature but on signaling channels for services like the Short Message Service (SMS).

Signaling information element confidentiality means the requirement to protect user related data on signaling channels. Such data includes the International Mobile

Equipment Identity (IMEI), the IMSI, the calling subscriber directory number, and the called subscriber directory number. This again is implemented using encryption.

2.1.3   Authentication and Encryption

GSM security has been designed as "security by obscurity", which means that the detailed algorithm specifications are not published in order to avoid anybody breaking them. Such a security scheme is obviously very dangerous, and it failed in 1998 when the authentication algorithms became public due to a leaked document. They can be found at (Smartcard Developer Association, 1998). The algorithm used for traffic encryption has been reverse-engineered by (Smartcard Developer Association, 1998) also in 1998.

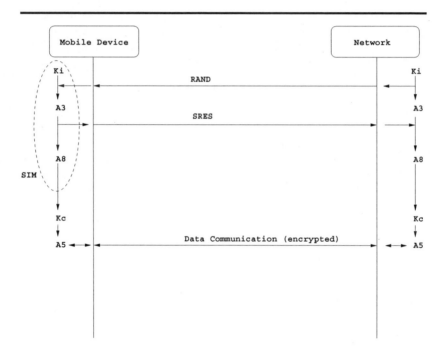

Figure 2.2: GSM Authentication and Encryption

Figure 2.2 shows an overview of GSM authentication and encryption as it is explained in (Brookson, 1994). The user's SIM holds a 128 bit shared key K_i that is also stored in the user's HLR's AUC. That key K_i is used to run a challenge-response based authentication between the mobile device and the network. It starts with a 128 bit challenge $RAND$ sent by the network which is processed using an algorithm A_3 to produce the 32 bit Signed RESponse ($SRES$), which is sent back.

The network is able to do the same calculations in order to be able to compare the expected $SRES$ with the received one. In case the values match, the $SRES$ will be processed further using an algorithm A_8 to calculate the 64 bit session key K_C used for traffic encryption with algorithm A_5. The algorithms A_3 and A_8 are running on the SIM, whereas A_5 is running outside the SIM.

The set of algorithms A_3/A_8 - also known as $COMP128$ - is known to be weak since 1998 (Smartcard Developer Association, 1998), but it is still in use. For traffic encryption, there are two algorithms in use today: $A_5/1$ and $A_5/2$. Both are still kept secret by the operators although they have been reverse-engineered. According to (ETSI, 1993a), an operator may also allow clear-text traffic in case mobile station and network do not have the same subset of supported algorithms A_5.

The subscriber always has to authenticate himself to his HLR's AUC even during roaming. As it would be unsafe to send the shared keys K_i over the network, operators exchange the values $RAND$, $SRES$, and K_C instead.

2.2 Third Generation Cellular Networks

UMTS stands for Universal Mobile Telecommunications System, which is the next generation mobile network following GSM with much higher data rates. It has been deployed since 2002 and will be replaced by Long Term Evolution (LTE) (3GPP, 2008) in the near future. UMTS allows for much higher data rates than those possible in GSM, but requires a completely new infrastructure that will be explained in the next section. UMTS allows for Circuit Switched (CS) services like those provided in GSM networks as well as Packet Switched (PS) IP based services. If GSM has been labeled as 2G network, UMTS can be referred to as 3G, and LTE as 4G.

The section starts with an overview of the UMTS architecture, goes on with the security considerations and ends with a short section about user authentication in UMTS.

2.2.1 Architecture

The UMTS network architecture is very similar to the GSM network shown in Section 2.1.1. Figure 2.3 shows all the important components of the network.

The *User Equipment (UE)*, which is the UMTS variant of the GSM's Mobile Station (MS), associates with a base station called *Node B*. Node B is a logical network entity responsible for the transmission and reception of data in one or more cells to and from the UE. Additionally, Node B is the gateway into the *Radio Network Subsystem (RNS)*. The second component of the RNS is the *Radio Network Controller (RNC)* which controls the use and the integrity of the radio resources. Behind the RNC stands the *Core Network (CN)* consisting of the *Mobile Switching Center (MSC)*, the *Visitor Location Register (VLR)*, the optional *Equipment Identity Register (EIR)*, the *Home Subscriber Server (HSS)*, and the *Serving GPRS Support Node (SGSN)*. Furthermore, there are two entities providing gateway functionality to other CNs: the *Gateway MSC (GMSC)* and the *Gateway GPRS Support Node (GGSN)*. The components needed to provide Circuit Switched (CS) services are the MSC, the EIR, and the HSS which actually consists of the *Home Location Register*

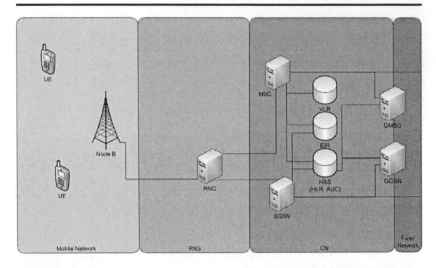

Figure 2.3: UMTS Network Overview. UE = User Equipment, RNS = Radio Network Subsystem, RNC = Radio Network Controller, CN = Core Network, MSC = Mobile Switching Center, HLR = Home Location Register, VLR = Visitor Location Register, EIR = Equipment Identity Register, AUC = Authentication Center, HSS = Home Subscriber Server, SGSN = Serving GPRS Support Node, GMSC = Gateway MSC, GGSN = Gateway GPRS Support Node.

(HLR) and the *Authentication Center (AUC)*. The functionality of these components is exactly the same as in GSM networks (see Section 2.1.1 for details). In order to route calls to another MSCs, the GMSC is used.

The Packet Switched (PS) domain of the network consists of the SGSN, the HSS, and the optional EIR. The SGSN stores all the subscription and location information for PS services and uses the HSS to authenticate UE. The Gateway that is responsible for routing PS calls to other SGNSs is the GGSN.

2.2.2   Security Considerations

The security features of UMTS are specified in (ETSI, 2009b). The document defines five security feature groups:

1. network access security,

2. network domain security,

3. user domain security,

4. application domain security, and

5. visibility and configuration potential of security.

Network access security covers the secure access to 3G services and defines functionality to protect against attacks against the radio access link. In order to ensure the confidentiality of the user's identity and her location, as well as her untraceability, (ETSI, 2009b) proposes to use temporary IDs that change from time to time. If the real identity needs to be sent over the network, it should always be encrypted. Furthermore, the user and the network should authenticate each other at each connection setup. In order to provide confidentiality for the subsequent data and signaling traffic, the authentication is followed by a cipher algorithm and key agreement. As user and signaling data should not only be confidential but also integrity protected, there is also an integrity algorithm and key agreement. Network access security may also include the identification of the mobile equipment, which requires sending the IMEI. As this method may be unprotected, fraud is possible here.

The features that provide security for the connection and signaling after a successful access are summarized as network domain security. Furthermore, this group deals with the protection against attacks on the wired network. The base for these algorithms is the algorithm and key agreement phase in the access part. It is also a task of the network domain security to provide a fraud information gathering system.

User domain security covers the secure access to mobile stations, which includes the authentication of the user at the Universal SIM (USIM - the SIM application for UMTS) and the authentication of the USIM at the User Equipment (UE). The user is authenticated using a PIN code that he is allowed to type in incorrectly only twice. If he gives a wrong pin in the third try, the USIM will be locked and can only be unlocked using a so called super PIN. In order to check whether an USIM is allowed to access a certain UE, USIM and UE also share a secret key.

The secure exchange of data by applications is summarized under application domain security. This covers the data exchange in the user as well as the provider domain and is restricted to applications installed on the USIM.

The fifth group called visibility and configuration potential of security summarizes functions provided to the user to inform herself whether a security feature is active or not and whether a service should have a certain security feature or not. (ETSI, 2009c) defines a ciphering indication feature that allows for visibility of security. Furthermore the user should be able to enable or disable the USIM authentication at least for certain services. Additionally it should be up to the user to accept or reject outgoing or incoming calls that are clear-text and she should be able to define the acceptable ciphering algorithms.

2.2.3 Authentication and Encryption

The UMTS authentication algorithm is based on a challenge-response protocol in order to be compatible with the GSM authentication shown in Section 2.1.3. The protocol itself does not rely on security by obscurity anymore. Instead the complete detailed description of the algorithms can be found in (ETSI, 2009b). But as these algorithms are not essential for this thesis, this section only describes the general message flow of the authentication protocol as shown in Figure 2.4.

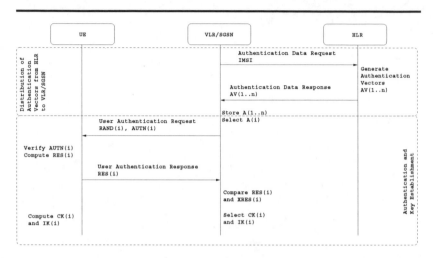

Figure 2.4: UMTS Authentication and Key Establishment

The authentication starts with an *authentication data request* containing the IMSI and the requesting node's type which may be either PS or CS. The HLR will then generate some authentication vectors $AV(1..n)$ that are equivalent to the GSM triplet. The HLR may also have pre-computed those vectors, each of them being good for one authentication and key agreement. The vectors are ordered based on a sequence number and include a 128 bit random number $RAND$, an expected response $XRES$, a 128 bit cipher key CK, an 128 bit integrity key IK, and an authentication token $AUTN$.

The HLR sends $AV(1..n)$ back to the VLR or SGSN who stores them locally. That phase is called distribution phase and is only needed in case the VLR or SGSN does not have any vectors anymore for a given UE.

During the authentication phase itself, the VLR or SGSN selects the next vector $AV(i)$ and sends $RAND(i)$ and $AUTN(i)$ to the UE. Based on 64 bit MAC that protects $AUTN(i)$, the UE is able to verify the $AUTN(i)$ value and computes $RES(i)$ out of $RAND(i)$ and $AUTN(i)$. Since the VLR or SGSN also received the $XRES(i)$ from the HLR, it may easily decide whether $RES(i)$ is correct or not. The authentication phase ends with the generation of $CK(i)$ and $IK(i)$ on the UE as well as the selection of the appropriate $CK(i)$ and $IK(i)$ at the VLR or SGSN.

As mentioned above, the detailed algorithms for computing RES, CK, and IK as well as AV are specified in (ETSI, 2009b).

In case the authentication fails, the VLR or SGSN should report that back to the HLR. Furthermore, if an UE moves from one VLR or SGSN to another one, old and new network access point may exchange the unused authentication vectors in order to reduce the requests for the HLR.

Lastly, if an UE wants to establish a connection, it can indicate the cipher and integrity algorithms it supports. In case there is no common subset between the network and the UE, it is up to the network whether it allows clear-text connections or not.

2.3 Interim Conclusion

This chapter has discussed the details of GSM and UMTS networks. It has been shown that although GSM and UMTS networks are rather complicated, they provide very good usability, since the user does not need to configure anything by herself. All she has to do is to buy a SIM card, insert the card into a mobile phone, switch on the phone and use it. This comfortable authentication scheme is realized by letting the user sign a contract that binds him to his SIM card. However, there are several drawbacks to GSM/ UMTS networks. First of all, they do not reach the high bandwidths of wireless LANs the users are used to, although LTE might help here in the near future. Furthermore, the device identity (the SIM) used to log in to the network is at the same time the primary identity - the mobile phone number - of the user within the network. If the user changes the SIM, she will not be available anymore under the same identity. Lastly, if a user decides to use several identities for different purposes, she has to buy several SIM cards, which usually results in several mobile phones, too. This is rather uncomfortable for a user. Chapter 3 shows how wireless LANs overcome the drawbacks of GSM/ UMTS networks except for the authentication.

3

Wireless Computer Networks

In February 1980, the Institute of Electrical and Electronics Engineering (IEEE) started to work on the IEEE 802 standards series dealing with local and metropolitan area networks. The name "802" was chosen for the starting date (2/80). Part 11 of IEEE 802 deals with wireless LANs and is described in this chapter. IEEE 802.11 (IEEE, 2007) specifies the medium access and physical layer requirements for wireless LANs and has been released in the first version in 1997 without any confidentiality algorithms. It was only in 1999 that Wired Equivalent Privacy (WEP) was added, and it took a long time until an authentication infrastructure like 802.1X (IEEE, 2004b) was added. One reason why IEEE 802.11 came without security and confidentiality algorithms was that the export of that technology out of the US was prohibited at the time the standard was written.

The sub-standards IEEE 802.11a, 802.11b, 802.11g, 802.11n, and 802.11p all deal with the physical layer and higher transmission speeds, whereas IEEE 802.11e deals with Quality of Service (QoS) and IEEE 802.11i finally with the integration of IEEE 802.1X into 802.11. Summarizing, the IEEE 802.11 series deals with the lower layers of the OSI model, whereas the upper layers are left to other (IEEE and Internet Engineering Task Force (IETF)) standards.

One characteristic of IEEE 802.11 LANs in contrast to wired IEEE 802 LANs is that wireless LANs (WLANs) are connection oriented. In IEEE 802.11, retransmission, checksums, and fragmentation are handled on the lower layers whereas other IEEE 802 technologies like Ethernet leave this functionality to the upper layers.

Nowadays, IEEE 802.11 starts to be seen as a replacement for GSM and UMTS networks since it provides all the same services, such as voice calls and messaging as well as comfort services like browsing etc. This chapter discusses architectural issues of IEEE 802.11 networks and compares them to GSM/ UMTS networks.

Notations

A **station** in IEEE 802.11 networks describes the client entity that accesses the network. A station associates itself with an **access point** that interconnects several stations or even links the WLAN to a backbone network. The **supplicant** is a logical component running on a station that requests authentication at an **authenticator**, which is usually running on the access point. The authenticator relays the authentication requests to an **authentication server** running in the backbone which does the decision making.

Lastly, this chapter talks about **authentication** and **authorization**. Authentication describes the process of confirming someone's identity, whereas authorization covers the application of access rights or policies. This chapter uses both terms as synonyms since authentication and authorization are usually done within the same step.

3.1 Architecture

The general goal of IEEE 802.11 was "to provide wireless connectivity to automatic machinery, equipment, or stations that require rapid development, which may be portable or hand-held, or which may be mounted on moving vehicles within a local area" (Hayes, 1996). The architecture that has been designed to meet that goal is described in this section, starts with a short overview of the terminology.

Mobile, portable, and fixed computers in IEEE 802.11 are called *stations*. The difference between a mobile and a portable station is that portable stations are disconnected when moving, whereas mobile stations move while being connected. Two or more stations form a so called *Basic Service Set (BSS)*. A BSS is always connected to a base called an *Access Point (AP)*, whereas an *Independent BSS (IBSS)* is a stand alone cell of equally equipped stations. An IBSS is also called an ad-hoc network. The backbone infrastructure connecting two or more BSSs is called *Distribution System (DS)*, the AP of a BSS being the entry point to the DS. Lastly, a complex network consisting of BSSs and DSs is called an *Extended Service Set (ESS)*. See Figure 3.1 for a visualization of the components just mentioned.

The DS in Figure 3.1 can be anything - starting from a simple point-to-point bridge between two APs to a bigger Ethernet backbone. IEEE 802.11 does only specify the functional requirements for a DS: A DS has to provide so-called *Station Services (SS)* and *Distribution System Services (DSS)*.

SS include authentication, de-authentication, MAC Service Data Unit (MSDU) delivery, and privacy. Authentication is needed since wireless LANs (WLANs) are wider distributed and less controlled than wired networks. Every station within the AP's range can connect to the network if there is no authentication at all. Authentication is only possible within one BSS, never over different BSSs. Furthermore, authentication is usually implemented between an AP and a station, or in the case of an IBSS, between stations. The first two authentication protocols of IEEE 802.11 are Open System Authentication and Shared Key Authentication. In an Open System Authentication, everybody who attempts to authenticate will receive authentication,

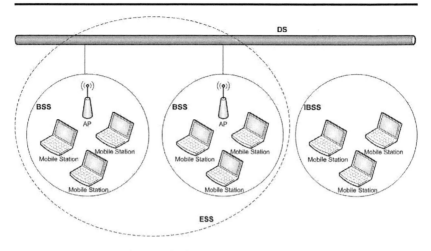

Figure 3.1: Architecture of 802.11 networks

which does obviously not provide any security at all. Shared Key Authentication has been implemented in Wired Equivalent Privacy (WEP) and proves that a user asking for authentication possesses a shared key distributed in advance. Furthermore, WEP implements a privacy that prevents eavesdropping in theory. In fact, WEP was already known to be weak at the time the standard was written. Lastly, SSs include de-authentication, which is needed when a station or an AP wants to terminate a session. De-authentication must always be followed by an automatic disassociation.

DSSs include association, re-association, disassociation, distribution, and integration. Re-/ Dis-/ Association deal with a station's mobility. There are three different types of mobility in IEEE 802.11:

1. No-transition mobility: The station does not move at all or moves only within its BSS.

2. BSS-transition mobility: A station moves between different BSSs within one ESS.

3. ESS-transition mobility: A station moves between different ESSs.

In no-transition mobility, a station associates itself with one BSS. Association describes the process of a station's affiliation with one BSS in order to get access to a LAN. In BSS-transition mobility, a node needs to re-associate itself with the AP of the destination BSS. Re-association allows a node to switch from one AP to another one. Re-association also includes dis-association from the first AP. ESS-transition mobility cannot be covered with simple re-association. This type of mobility requires the node to fully re-initiate the connection within the new ESS.

The DSS distribution service covers the transmission of data from the sender to the intended receiver. If a station wants to transmit data, it will send the packets to its AP, which will forward the traffic to the DS if needed. The DS will then address the so called output AP which forwards the packets to the destination node. If the output AP is a gateway to another type of IEEE 802 network, this process is called integration.

3.2   Security Considerations

The goal of IEEE 802.11 was to ensure that an intruder would not be able to access network resources simply by using WLAN equipment and that she would not be able to capture wireless traffic. In short, a WLAN should provide the same level of security as a wired LAN does.

The first approach to meeting those goals has been specified in (IEEE, 2007) and is called Wired Equivalent Privacy (WEP). WEP is based on RSA's RC4 (RSA Security, 2009) algorithm and is initialized using a shared secret that must be known by every station of a BSS. This secret is fed into a Pseudo Random Generator (PRNG) which outputs a key sequence of random bits equal in length to the largest possible packet. The sequence is then combined with every incoming and outgoing packet.

Since WEP was already known to be weak right from the beginning, the IEEE did release new security and authentication standards over the last years, called IEEE 802.1X (IEEE, 2004b) and IEEE 802.11i (IEEE, 2004a). IEEE 802.1X defines an authentication infrastructure, whereas IEEE 802.11i specifies the usage of IEEE 802.1X in IEEE 802.11 networks. Both standards are explained in more detail in the next sections.

3.2.1   An Authentication Framework

IEEE 802.1X defines a Port Access Control Protocol (PACP) with a port being the single point of attachment of a station to the LAN infrastructure. A port can be either a real physical port like in IEEE 802 Ethernet, or a logical port like an IEEE 802.11 association between a station and an AP. An entity associated with a port like a station or an AP (that is the authenticator) is called a Port Access Entity (PAE) in IEEE 802.1X. The general purpose of port access control is to refuse access to an unauthorized station (a supplicant in IEEE 802.1X terminology) and to prevent a station to connect to an unauthorized authenticator or network. IEEE 802.1X defines the general setup of port access control but does not define the authentication protocol itself.

One basic assumption of IEEE 802.1X is that one supplicant is connected to one authenticator PAE with the supplicant PAE being the entity that wishes to access the service behind a port and the authenticator PAE the one that wishes to enforce authentication before allowing a supplicant to access services behind that port. There is usually an authentication server located behind the authenticator that performs the actual authentication based on the supplicant's credentials and decides whether or not to allow access for that supplicant.

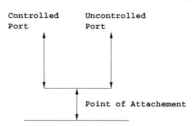

Figure 3.2: 802.1X Port Concept

Figure 3.2 shows the port concept. It consists of an uncontrolled port that allows the exchange of PDUs regardless of the authorization state whereas the controlled port allows the exchange only if it is in the authorized state. Both controlled and uncontrolled port share the same point of attachment to the network infrastructure. A PAE is only attached to one of the ports at a time. The supplicant PAE will change from the uncontrolled port to the controlled port after a successful authentication whereas the authenticator PAE is only connected to the uncontrolled port.

The controlled port has a state called *AuthControlledPortStatus* which can be either *authorized*, or *unauthorized*. Furthermore, there is the *AuthControlledPort-Control* parameter, which is used to administrate control over the port's authorization status. Possible values for *AuthControlledPortControl* are *ForceUnauthorized*, *ForceAuthorized*, and *auto* with *auto* being the default that makes the status dependent on the result of an authentication protocol.

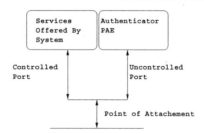

Figure 3.3: 802.1X Ports and Their Services

Figure 3.3 gives an overview of the different ports and services protected by IEEE 802.1X. As already mentioned, the supplicant PAE and the authenticator PAE communicate via the uncontrolled port, whereas services are only accessible via the controlled port. Authorization for the controlled port may be either in one (the incoming) direction or both. Unidirectional authorization allows services like wake-up on LAN that must run before any authorization may take place.

The task of the supplicant PAE is to supply information to an authenticator that will establish its credentials, but this information will only be sent in response to a request sent by the authenticator. The authenticator PAE will then forward this information to a suitable authentication server, which may be either co-located with the authenticator or separated. It is up to the authenticator PAE to implement the aging out of authorization and to request the supplicant to re-authenticate.

The authorization protocol that runs between supplicant PAE and authenticator PAE is the Port Access Control Protocol (PACP) itself in IEEE 802.1X terminology. The only payload of PACP is the EAP protocol discussed in Chapter 4. It is up to the EAP method to decide whether mutual authentication or one-way authentication is used.

Mutual authentication is supported by implementing the port concept on the supplicant as well. That means the supplicant also has an uncontrolled and a controlled port. In former versions of IEEE 802.1X, where only the authenticator had those ports, it was possible for a supplicant to connect to a rogue authenticator even if a mutual EAP method was used. This was possible due to the missing controlled port on the supplicant's side.

Besides mutual authentication where the supplicant has its own controlled port, there is also the possibility for a device to implement the supplicant and the authenticator role in order to implement some kind of bi-directional authentication. It has to be mentioned that bi-directional authentication is not the same as mutual authentication since the two sessions are not coupled. However, there are certain use cases where it might make sense to use bi-directional authentication rather than mutual authentication:

- One might wish to use separate keying material for each direction, but there is only an unidirectional keying algorithm available.

- There are different credentials for different roles.

- If two bridges are interconnected, they may have authorization requirements that can only be enforced by an authenticator.

Since PACP carries EAP, and EAP does not define any packets specific to the underlying network, IEEE 802.1X defines a new protocol that encapsulates EAP packets in IEEE 802 environments called EAP Over LAN (EAPOL). Besides carrying the actual EAP packets, EAPOL may also carry certain alert messages over the unauthorized port. That message type is called *EAPOL-Encapsulated-ASF-Alert* (ASF is short for Alerting Standards Format (DMTF, 2003)). It is up to other standards to specify the actual alert syntax and semantics. Furthermore, EAPOL knows the following packet types:

- *EAP-Packet*: As the name suggests, an EAPOL packet of this type carries an EAP packet.

- *EAPOL-Start*: This packet signals the start of an EAP authentication.

- *EAPOL-Logoff*: By sending this packet, the supplicant signals its desire to log off from the authenticator. If an authenticator wants to finish a session it has to time out the supplicant's authentication.

- *EAPOL-Key*: EAPOL may transmit its own keys in addition to the keys generated in EAP itself. This packet is optional.

Even if IEEE 802.1X specifies a protocol to carry EAP and requires EAP to be used for authentication, this standard does not specify EAP itself. The definition of EAP and EAP methods is left to other standardization bodies like the IETF as mentioned in Chapter 4.

Besides EAPOL there is another protocol needed in IEEE 802.1X to carry the authentication information between the authenticator and the authentication server. As will be mentioned in Chapter 4, EAPOL is used only between supplicant and authenticator. Between authenticator and authentication server, a so called Authentication, Authorization, and Accounting (AAA) protocol like RADIUS (Rigney *et al.*, 2000) or DIAMETER (Calhoun *et al.*, 2003) has to be used, which will be discussed in Chapter 4. Therefore the authenticator PAE does not only have to relay EAP packets between the supplicant and the authentication server, it must also re-pack EAP frames from EAPOL to AAA.

State Machines

IEEE 802.1X defines several state machines for several protocol entities, but only the authenticator and the supplicant state machine will be presented in this thesis since these two are important for the implementation.

Figure 3.4 shows the authenticator PAE state machine.

The first state entered is the *INITIALIZE* state. The authenticator will run the initialization procedure while remaining in that state and switch to *DISCON-NECTED* afterwards. *DISCONNECTED* means that the port is in the unauthorized state. The authenticator PAE will switch to *RESTART* if a new supplicant wants to authenticate or if an existing one needs to be asked for re-authentication. During the *RESTART* state, the authenticator informs the higher layers like EAP about the restart. When EAP acknowledges the restart, *CONNECTING* is entered. When EAP finally starts, the authenticator PAE switches to *AUTHENTICATING*. This state has three possible following states:

1. *ABORTING*, if too many timeouts happen. If an EAPOL-Start is received while in this state, *RESTART* will be entered again. However, if the supplicant gives up and sends EAPOL-Logoff, the authenticator will transition to *DISCONNECTED*.

2. *AUTHENTICATED*, if EAP finishes successfully. The port is now in the authorized state and the supplicant authenticated. In case a re-authentication is needed, the authenticator switches back to *RESTART*, whereas if the supplicant sends an EAPOL-Logoff, *DISCONNECTED* is entered.

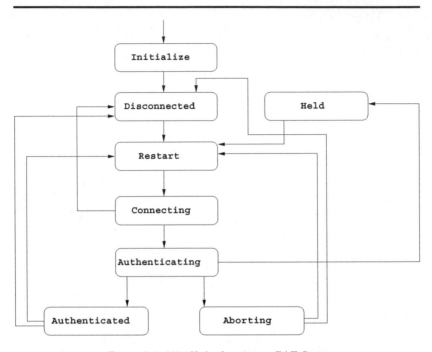

Figure 3.4: 802.1X Authenticator PAE States

3. *HELD*, if EAP results in EAP-Failure. While in this state, the authenticator discards any EAPOL packet in order to avoid brute-force attacks and the port is in the unauthorized state. After a certain timeout, *RESTART* will be entered again.

Those are the states and transitions of the authenticator PAE. Figure 3.5 shows the states and transitions of the supplicant PAE.

The supplicant starts either in the *LOGOFF* or the *DISCONNECTED* state. Afterwards it enters the *CONNECTING* state if it desires to connect and authenticate to an authenticator. In case the authenticator does not reply to authentication requests, the supplicant assumes that the authenticator is not EAPOL aware and enters the *AUTHENTICATED* state immediately. In case an EAP request is received, the supplicant transitions to *RESTART* and goes on to *AUTHENTICATING* if an EAP result is received. If the result was EAP-Success, *AUTHENTICATED* is entered, whereas EAP-Failure results in the transition to *HELD*. Another possibility to enter *HELD* is from *CONNECTING* if no authenticator can be acquired. *HELD* can be left to *CONNECTING* by timeout or to *RESTART* if another EAP request packet is received.

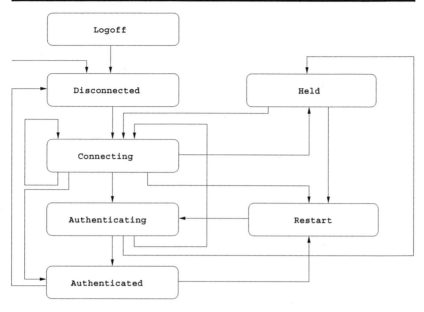

Figure 3.5: 802.1X Supplicant PAE States

Security Considerations

There are several attacks on IEEE 802.1X that have to be dealt with. This section covers only the main attacks mentioned in IEEE 802.1X.

The first one is called *Piggybacking* and means that one station authenticates correctly and therefore causes the port to open, while some other station uses the port instead of the authenticated one. IEEE 802.1X requires the authenticator to detect multiple stations on one port in order to prevent this type of attack. Today this type of attack is possible in wired networks, whereas wireless networks prevent it by using fast re-authentication.

Furthermore, there may be rogue authenticators a supplicant connects to, if no mutual authentication is used. Therefore, IEEE 802.1X recommends to use mutual authentication whenever possible. Next, IEEE 802.1X does not provide protection against snooping attacks. That must be done by the EAP method. Lastly, there is an attack called *cross talk* where one supplicant tries to send control packets to another supplicant in order for instance to disconnect the other supplicant. Such packets must be blocked by the authenticator.

3.2.2 How to Integrate the Authentication Framework into the Network Architecture

In 2001, the IEEE 802.1X standard, which covers the port access control described in the last section, has been released, but this standard does not specify how to use this authentication infrastructure in IEEE 802.11 networks. This integration is specified in IEEE 802.11i (IEEE, 2004a), released in 2004. Additionally, IEEE 802.11i defines the security association management protocols called *4-Way Handshake* and *Group Key Handshake*.

In short, the 4-Way Handshake is used to confirm the mutual possession of a Pairwise Master Key (PMK) and allows distributing a Group Temporal Key (GTK). A "group" in IEEE 802.11i describes an BSS or IBSS. The Group Key Handshake issues new GTKs to peers that have already formed a security association with the access point.

Robust Security Network Associations

IEEE 802.11i uses the notion of Robust Security Networks (RSN), which describes networks with certain security features. A RSN Association (RSNA) defines a number of security features in addition to WEP and the very basic IEEE 802.11 authentication. Those features include enhanced authentication mechanisms for stations, key management algorithms, the establishment of cryptographic keys, and enhanced data encapsulation mechanisms.

A RSNA uses IEEE 802.1X together with the newly defined protocols TKIP (Temporal Key Integrity Protocol) and CCMP (based on IETF CCM (Whiting *et al.*, 2003)) for access control. Key management is done using IEEE 802.1X EAPOL-Key frames, and confidentiality and data integrity are provided using RSN key management with TKIP and CCMP.

A RSNA has six strong requirements:

1. Each station has a reliable source of randomness.

2. Only mutual EAP methods are used.

3. Only strong mutual EAP methods must be used.

4. There is a trustworthy channel between authenticator and authentication server. IEEE 802.11i proposes to use RADIUS (Rigney *et al.*, 2000) or DIAMETER (Calhoun *et al.*, 2003) for that purpose.

5. An authentication server will never expose keying material to any other party than the authenticator.

6. An authenticator and a station will never expose keying material as well.

It has to be mentioned that a RSNA forbids the use of shared keys.

In IEEE 802.11i a *station* is the entity that implements the IEEE 802.1X supplicant PAE, whereas an *access point* implements the authenticator PAE. In case of an IBSS, all stations have to implement both rules.

The protocols TKIP and CCMP are replacements for WEP with the requirement that TKIP is implementable on devices that support WEP so far. All three protocols provide confidentiality, authentication and access control on Layer 2 of the OSI model.

If a station wants to connect to an IEEE 802.11i secured network, it has to discover the access point's (AP's) security settings first. This may be done by listening to beacons frequently sent by the AP or by actively asking the AP. If the security settings are acceptable, the supplicant starts the authentication by sending an EAPOL-Start which results in an EAP-request sent by the AP. EAP runs now over the IEEE 802.1X uncontrolled port. A successful EAP authentication ends with the generation of the so called Pairwise Master Key (PMK) on the authentication server and the supplicant. The authentication server will transmit the PMK to the AP over a secure channel. Last of all, the 4-Way Handshake shown in Figure 3.6 runs.

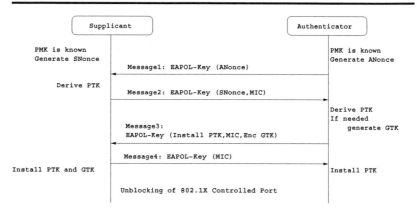

Figure 3.6: 802.11i 4-Way Handshake

As the name suggests, the protocol consists of only 4 messages. After having generated and transmitted the PMK, supplicant and authenticator generate a nonce each, which is exchanged and is needed to generate the Pairwise Transient Key (PTK). Beside the nonces, the function for generating the PTK needs the authenticator address (AA), the supplicant address (SA), and the PMK. All those parameters are fed into a Pseudo Random Function (PRF):

$$PTK = PRF(PMK, AA, SA, ANonce, SNonce)$$

The PTK is then split into five keys:

1. A temporal encryption key,

2. two temporal Message Integrity Code (MIC) keys,

3. the EAPOL-Key encryption key (KEK), and

4. the EAPOL-Key confirmation key (KCK).

In case the authentication was not done using EAP, but using a pre-shared key (PSK), the 4-Way Handshake also includes the generation and exchange of the Group Transient Key (GTK) out of a Group Master Key (GMK).

Last of all, the IEEE 802.1X controlled port is unblocked and the supplicant can access all the services protected by IEEE 802.11i.

Figure 3.7: 802.11i Group Key Protocol

In case authentication using a PSK is used, the Group Key Handshake protocol shown in Figure 3.7 allows to update GTKs during an open session.

While the PTK generated during the 4-Way Handshake is used to protect unicast traffic, the GTK will be used to protect multicast and broadcast traffic.

The distribution of the client authentication credentials for EAP or the PSK is out of scope of IEEE 802.11i.

Furthermore, IEEE 802.11i defines the authentication procedure also for IBSSs, but as those are out of scope of this thesis, the interested reader should have a look at (IEEE, 2004a).

3.3   Device Identification

IEEE standards like IEEE 802.1X (IEEE, 2004b) or IEEE 802.11i (IEEE, 2004a) define how to authenticate users in IEEE 802.11 networks, but so far, there was no common device identifier like the IMEI in GSM. IEEE 802.1AR (IEEE, 2009), which has been specified in 2009, defines a secure device identifier.

The main motivation for defining a secure device identifier was that there are a lot of devices that are designed for unattended autonomous operation like routers and bridges. So far, these devices remained mostly unauthenticated, which poses a threat to the device itself as well as to the network.

The general purpose of (IEEE, 2009) was to define a globally unique device identifier as well as the management and the cryptographic binding of a device to its identifier(s). Furthermore the standard aims to specify the relationship between an initially installed identifier and subsequent locally significant identities that can be used as synonyms of the initially installed identifier (ID). Lastly, IEEE 802.1AR defines interfaces and methods for using device identifiers (DevIDs) with existing and new provisioning and authentication protocols like IEEE 802.1X.

In order to meet the goals mentioned above, IEEE 802.1AR specifies a DevID which is "cryptographically bound to a device and supports the authentication of the device's identity" (IEEE, 2009). In general a DevID consists of a DevID secret and a DevID X.509 credential. In order to be able to use different identifiers for different purposes, it is possible to generate so called locally significant identifiers (LDevIDs) that may be associated with the manufacturer's initially provided DevID. Those LDevIDs may then be used in authentication protocols. In case a user cannot use LDevIDs to preserve privacy, she is able to disable the DevID completely.

The need for an initial DevID (IDevID) may result in a costly pre-provisioning process that often needs user interaction, but is necessary to ensure the cryptographic binding. Furthermore, it has to be ensured that every device has only one single IDevID.

In order for LDevIDs to provide the same level of security as the IDevIDs, they must be bound to the device in a way that makes it impossible to forge them or to transfer them to another device without the knowledge of the private key. Such a requirement leads to a secure DevID module which is able to store and operate DevID secrets and credentials in a secure way. That module should store the entire credential chain up to the (manufacturer's) root credential.

Whereas the LDevIDs may have a short lifetime, the lifetime of the IDevID is unlimited respectively as long as the lifetime of the device itself. That underlines the need for a really secure storage and use of that initial DevID.

Besides storing all the credentials and secrets, the DevID module must support asymmetric cryptography, hash algorithms, a random number generator, signing, the enabling and disabling of DevID credentials and keys as well as the generation, insertion and deleting of LDevID keys. Furthermore, the module must ensure that secrets are never revealed to anyone, as well as the integrity of all the data kept inside the module.

The IEEE 802.1AR does also describe some usage scenarios for DevIDs: One of the possible applications of a DevID might be EAP-TLS (Simon *et al.*, 2008) although the ciphersuite has to be set to TLS_DHE_RSA_WITH_AES_128_CBC_SHA since DevIDs can only be used for signing operations. The nonces used during the TLS handshake should be generated using the DevID module's RNG. Furthermore, a DevID might be used in an enterprise environment to enroll devices to the local security infrastructure.

3.4   Interim Conclusion

As already mentioned in the introduction to this chapter, IEEE 802.11 wireless networks can be seen somehow as replacements of GSM/ UMTS networks. GSM has been designed for Circuit Switched (CS) services like voice calls, whereas UMTS does already provide Packet Switched (PS) services like IP based applications. Compared to wireless networks, however UMTS networks are very limited in data rates and therefore in comfort.

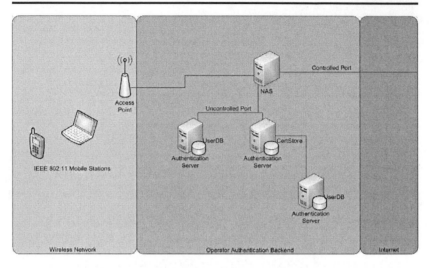

Figure 3.8: WLAN Architecture Complete

Figure 3.8 shows a general overview of the IEEE 802.11 network architecture presented in this chapter. Recalling the GSM architecture presented in Figure 2.1, there are some components that exist in both architectures. There is for instance the access point, which is comparable to the Base Transceiver Station (BTS). The functionality of the GSM Authentication Center (AUC) is distributed between the NAS and the authentication servers. The authentication server responsible for a certain user can be seen as Home Location Register (HLR) since it stores the user's credentials. However, IEEE 802.11 does not know the location of a user. That is due to the fact that the routing of services like chat is based on the user's ID for that service and not on her network ID. Furthermore, with all the additional standards like IEEE 802.11i and IEEE 802.1X that aim to make the original IEEE 802.11 more usable in public setups, the setup became even more similar to the GSM/ UMTS network and so should the user experience. WLANs do now cover all the components that are necessary for a public commercial roll-out, namely authentication services, roaming services as mentioned in IEEE 802.11r (IEEE, 2008), and even Quality of Service (QoS) specified in IEEE 802.11e (IEEE, 2005). With the emergence of IEEE 802.1AR, there is also a standardized device identity comparable to the IMEI in GSM/ UMTS networks. However there is still no specific authentication protocol proposal with IEEE 802.11 hardware only to be used in public wireless networks which weakens the user experience. Chapter 4 will discuss authentication protocols used today and their drawbacks, whereas Chapter 6 will show how to use the TPMs presented in Chapter 5 to implement an authentication protocol as secure and comfortable as in GSM/ UMTS networks.

4

Authentication In Wireless Computer Networks

By definition, wireless LANs are more open than wired networks. The access to wired networks can be limited by the number of network outlets, whereas wireless networks can be accessed by anybody in range. Authentication in wireless networks is therefore a very important topic even for private wireless networks. However, if pre-shared keys are perfectly sufficient for private WLANs, public wireless networks need a real device and/ or user authentication as well as an accounting infrastructure. That is due to the fact that public wireless networks are usually operated by professional Internet Service Providers (ISPs) that will hardly allow access for free.

In order to implement an authentication, authorization, and accounting (AAA) infrastructure for public wireless networks, three protocols have been developed:

1. EAPOL, which has been explained in the previous chapter. EAPOL runs between the client that wants to be authenticated – the supplicant – and the access point – the authenticator. EAPOL carries the EAP protocol.

2. AAA protocols that run between the authenticator and the back-end authentication server.

3. EAP protocols, which is short for extensible authentication protocol, run between the supplicant and the authentication server.

This chapter starts with an introduction and discussion of EAP protocols and then discusses RADIUS and DIAMETER.

4.1 Captive Portals

Captive Portals – also called Sticky Pages – are authentication web pages used on public wireless hotspots for instance at universities or in a city WLAN.

Figure 4.1 shows the captive portal page of the university of Fribourg. Those portals turn the web browser into an authentication device by blocking any traffic except HTTP and HTTPS for new clients. Furthermore, the first HTTP/ HTTPS

Figure 4.1: Captive Portal Page University of Fribourg

request is redirected to the captive portal page in order to force the user to give his credentials. This page has to be stored on the gateway itself or on a white-listed server in order to be available right from the beginning. After the user's credentials have been verified, the gateway is informed to white-list the client for every protocol and destination.

Captive portals are very easy to use since they do not require any special configuration on the client, which is why they are the most common authentication method on public wireless hotspots in universities, hotels etc. However, they do have limitations regarding security and usability, as is shown in the next sections.

4.1.1   Security Considerations

Captive portals that rely on HTTP redirection have to allow DNS requests to pass the gateway even before an user is authenticated. This allows to circumvent the captive portal using so called "DNS tunneling". As described in (DNS Tunnel, 2009), one has to setup a fake server that serves as translation gateway between the DNS tunnel and the Internet. It is obvious that one will not achieve great performance using a DNS tunnel, but at least it is for free. This DNS tunneling attack may be prevented by redirecting the DNS traffic too. An operator might redirect every DNS request to its own DNS server and reply to any DNS request with the IP of the captive portal, which renders the attack useless.

However, there is another threat for the network since the client is identified by his IP or MAC address, which is too weak. An attacker might snoop all the traffic and steal the client's IP and/ or MAC address to get free access. This attack cannot really be avoided without additional software on the client such as VPN clients.

4.1.2 Interim Conclusion

Besides the security issues mentioned above, captive portals are uncomfortable due to several facts. First of all, one has to open a browser before doing anything else at every first connect. Second - and that is even more problematic - it requires a full web browser on the device that is used, which is not possible on embedded devices like gaming consoles. There is usually no possibility to automate the access since the portal pages are normally full of advertisements and therefore subject to frequent changes. However, concluding one can say that captive portals are a good fallback if no other authentication method is available, but they should be only used as a fallback.

4.2 The Extensible Authentication Protocol (EAP)

The Extensible Authentication Protocol (EAP) has been defined in RFC 3748 (Aboba *et al.*, 2004) and RFC 5247 (Aboba *et al.*, 2008). The basic idea of EAP is to provide an authentication framework supporting multiple authentication methods called EAP methods in an easily extensible manner. EAP methods implement specific authentication protocols inside the EAP framework. One example is EAP-TLS which implements the TLS protocol inside EAP and will be discussed in Section 4.2.3. EAP runs over data link layers like the Point-to-Point Protocol (PPP) or IEEE 802 without the need for the Internet Protocol (IP). Duplicate elimination and retransmissions are handled by EAP itself whereas the packet ordering should be ensured by the lower layer. Fragmentation is not provided by EAP nor required to be done by the lower layer. Instead, EAP methods that want to make use of fragmentation have to implement it themselves.

─────────────────── **Notations** ───────────────────

The protocols described in this section consist more or less of the same protocol entities but due to historical reasons those entities have different names in every protocol or are even named differently within the same protocol specification.

In Transport Layer Security (TLS), it is always the **client** that wants to be authenticated to a network and will therefore connect to a **server**. In the Extensible Authentication Protocol (EAP) the client is named **EAP peer** and the endpoint of that authentication within the network is called **EAP server**. The EAP server itself may reside on the **authenticator** which is the access point a peer associates with or on a **back-end authentication server** in case the authenticator acts as pass-through authenticator. In general, when speaking about a **client** or **peer** within this section, it is always the entity that wants to be authenticated to the network. When speaking about a **server** the author always means the authentication endpoint within the network. Last of all, a **supplicant** is the authentication software running on the peer.

───

Figure 4.2 shows the EAP architecture. There is always an EAP peer – also called supplicant – that wants to be authenticated and an authenticator the peer

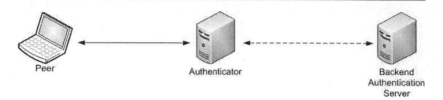

Figure 4.2: EAP Architecture

connects to. The authenticator may provide authentication methods itself or it may act as pass-through to the back-end authentication server.

Even if this architecture looks rather simple, a real setup can be of arbitrary complexity as can be seen in Figure 4.3. All entities involved in the EAP setup can communicate over different ports: the peer may be connected to more than one authenticator and the authenticator itself may be connected to more than one authentication server, be it for load balancing or for backup reasons.

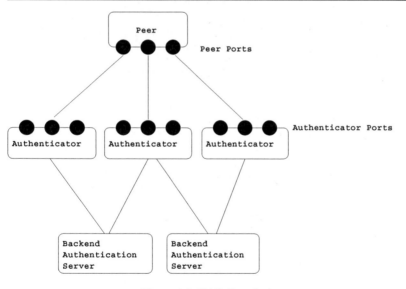

Figure 4.3: EAP Complexity

EAP methods should support key derivation in order to secure subsequent data communication, which leads to three phases during peer authentication:

- Phase 0: Discovery

- Phase 1: Authentication

  - Phase 1a: EAP Authentication
  - Phase 1b: AAA Key Transport (optional)

- Phase 2: Secure Association Protocol

  - Phase 2a: Unicast Secure Association
  - Phase 2b: Multicast Secure Association (optional)

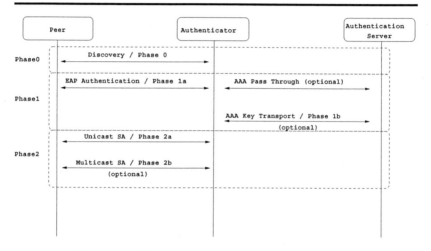

Figure 4.4: EAP Phases when supporting Key Derivation

Figure 4.4 shows the scope of each phase. Phase 0 is initiated by the peer to locate authenticators and discover their abilities. In IEEE 802.11 based networks, peers can query for access points by sending a probe request that will be answered with the access point's (AP's) Service Set Identifiers (SSIDs) and its authentication capabilities. After having found a suitable access point – the authenticator – phase 1a starts, where the peer tries to connect to the AP, which causes the EAP conversation to start. The conversation takes place between EAP peer and server, where the server is either the authenticator or the back-end authentication server depending on which method is available where. Usually the conversation starts with an identity request sent by the authenticator, which may be omitted in case the peer's identity is predetermined. After the peer has answered with his identity, a sequence of method specific request response messages follows as long as needed. As EAP is a so-called lock-step protocol, new requests can only be sent after having received a valid response. Retransmissions of requests can be done if there was no response within a certain timeout but should stop after a suitable number of retries. The conversation ends when the EAP server is able to authenticate the peer – resulting in an *EAP Success* message – or when the server decides that he cannot authenticate the peer – resulting in an *EAP Failure* message. The decision of the server is usually based on authentication and authorization aspects.

As outlined above, EAP authentication is always initiated by the server or the authenticator sending the initial request whereas many non-EAP authentication protocols are initiated by the peer. However, these protocols may be easily implemented within EAP by adding one or two messages in the beginning. Furthermore, EAP authentication may consist of a sequence of EAP methods but it is not allowed to mix two or more methods. That means that every authentication method must run without interference by others.

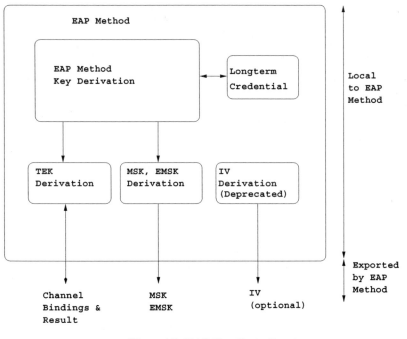

Figure 4.5: EAP Key Derivation

Many EAP methods generate keying material in phase 1a to be used to secure the subsequent communication. Figure 4.5 shows the three key relevant parameters exported by those methods:

- an initialization vector (IV) of at least 64 octets, but as it is a well-known value in methods like EAP-TLS, the IV is now deprecated,

- a Master Session Key (MSK) with a length of at least 64 octets and an Extended Master Session Key (EMSK) that is reserved for future use,

- transient EAP keys (TEKs), which are used for instance to deploy cryptographic channel binding of the lower layer ciphersuites.

It is up to the EAP method to ensure the freshness of the (E)MSK even if either the peer or the authentication server does not have a high quality random number generator. In case the peer is mobile and changes the authenticator, back-end authentication servers may track and analyze the peer's movements and transport the keys to the authenticator in a pro-active manner. If the peer arrives at the new authenticator, there is no need for a complete authentication but only for a proof of possession of those keys. It has to be mentioned that the EAP method has to ensure that the long-term credentials are still valid (also applies for fast re-authentication) since credentials like smart cards may have been removed.

In case the EAP server runs on the back-end authentication server, the keying material derived in phase 1a has to be transmitted to the authenticator using an AAA protocol like RADIUS or DIAMETER (phase 1b), which will be discussed in Section 4.3.

When the authenticator has all the keying material needed to secure the communication with the peer, it will establish a Unicast Security Association (SA) with the peer (phase 2a). In case Multicast is supported and requested, authenticator and peer have to negotiate a Multicast SA instead (phase 2b).

Aside from naming the entities to allow the definition of the scope of EAP keying material, the SA includes a mutual proof of possession of the EAP keying material and a secure capabilities negotiation in order to ensure that no downgrading attack has happened. Furthermore, the SA allows to generate the Transient Session Keys (TSKs) that will be used with the selected ciphersuite to protect the subsequent data communication. Figure 4.6 shows the different TSK derivation "algorithms" for IEEE 802.11i and IEEE 802.1X. Whereas IEEE 802.1X uses the complete MSK to derive the TSK, IEEE 802.11i uses only the first half of the MSK. Furthermore, IEEE 802.11i (IEEE, 2004a) implements phase 2a and b in its 4-way handshake.

Additionally, the SA supports key caching, key lifetime management and key state and scope synchronization between peer and authenticator. Last but not least peer and authenticator have to negotiate a traffic profile since source and destination address of both may differ on lower layers.

EAP has four invariants that have to be fulfilled in every implementation:

1. Mode independence: the peer should not realize whether he is authenticating to an authenticator running his own authentication server or whether the authenticator is running in pass-through mode.

2. Media independence: as already mentioned, EAP methods should not rely on lower layer characteristics that exceed ordering and error detection.

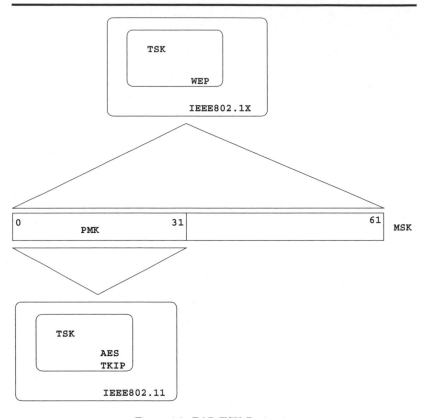

Figure 4.6: EAP TSK Derivation

3. Method independence: the authenticator does not to implement EAP methods as long as the authentication server does it.

4. Ciphersuite independence: the EAP keying material has to be large enough to handle any ciphersuite. This invariant is a result of media independence since lower layer ciphersuites vary between different media.

The next section goes into the details of the EAP authentication framework as these are the basics for EAP methods like TLS and SIM explained below.

4.2.1   Authentication Details

There are several layers involved in EAP authentication, as can be seen in Figure 4.7.

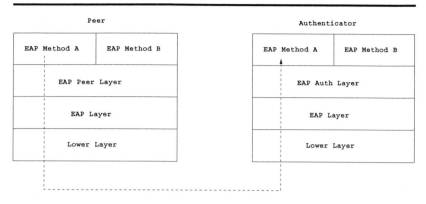

Figure 4.7: EAP Layer

The EAP method layer on top of the stack represents the implemented authentication algorithm. As EAP does not support path MTU discovery, fragmentation will be implemented on that layer too, if needed. Below the method layer lie the peer and authenticator layers. Usually the peer implements the peer layer and the authenticator the authenticator later, but some hosts will implement both layers as will be shown later. The peer and authenticator layer demultiplex incoming EAP packets according to their code field (see Figure 4.9 for details about the packet format). There are four different code values:

1 request packet

2 response packet

3 success packet

4 failure packet

Packets with the code number 1, 3, and 4 are delivered to the peer layer, whereas code number 2 will be delivered to the authenticator layer.

The next lower layer is the EAP layer which transmits and receives EAP packets over the lower layer and implements duplicate detection and retransmission. Finally, the lowest layer is a data link layer like IEEE 802 that simply transmits and receives EAP frames between peer and authenticator. The data link layer is assumed to be unreliable, which is why EAP supports retransmissions, but it has to provide error detection and ordering. The detailed interaction between the EAP and the lower layer is highly implementation dependent.

According to RFC 3748 (Aboba *et al.*, 2004), it is not mandatory for an EAP implementation to follow that model but it has to behave as if the implementation would follow it.

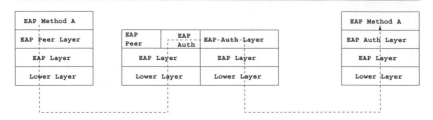

Figure 4.8: EAP Layer With Pass-Through Authenticator

Figure 4.8 shows the layers on a pass-through authenticator.

The pass-through authenticator processes packets up to the peer – checking the code, identifier and length fields – and authentication layer, but instead of doing the method specific processing, it forwards the packets into the right direction. Therefore there is usually no need for a method layer. In case the authenticator provides some local EAP methods, there has to be a method layer anyway and the pass through authenticator will check the type field too, to determine how to handle the packet.

It has to be mentioned that RADIUS and DIAMETER do not allow for pass-through peers, which is why the authenticator cannot take the role of the peer towards the authentication server.

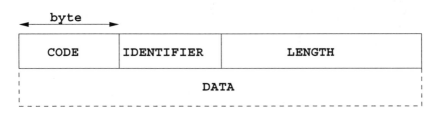

Figure 4.9: EAP Packet Format

The general format of an EAP packet is shown in Figure 4.9. As already mentioned, the code field interpretation on the EAP layer is very similar to the protocol number in IP and is used to decide whether a packet should be delivered to the peer or the authenticator. On the method layer, the code number will be used to process the packet further. Furthermore, the code field defines the format of the data field that may be zero or more bytes in length. The identifier byte is only used to match responses with requests. One byte is obviously a bit short to ensure uniqueness in an EAP conversation of unknown length, but EAP only requires the identifier of a request to be different from the previous request and not to be unique. The value should be initialized with a random number at the beginning of an EAP conversation in order to avoid sequence attacks. If a request packet has to be retransmitted it will use the same identifier value in order to distinguish it from new ones. The length of the complete message shown in Figure 4.9 is summed up in the length field.

Packets with a code number of 3 or 4 are quite easy to process. They either lead to the negotiation of a SA in case of number 3 (success) or stop the authentication in case of number 4 (failure). Furthermore, in contrast to request and response packets, success and failure packets are of a very simple format as can be seen in Figure 4.10.

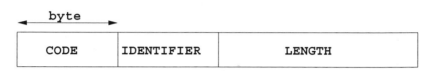

Figure 4.10: EAP Success/Failure Packet Format

Success and failure packets will never be retransmitted in case they are lost. Instead, a timeout will occur, which causes the authentication to start over again. Furthermore, a success packet will only be accepted in the matching protocol state in order to prevent Denial of Service (DoS) attacks on the peer.

Request and response messages are method dependent and may carry data depending on their type. Therefore, their format is a bit more complicated as shown in Figure 4.11.

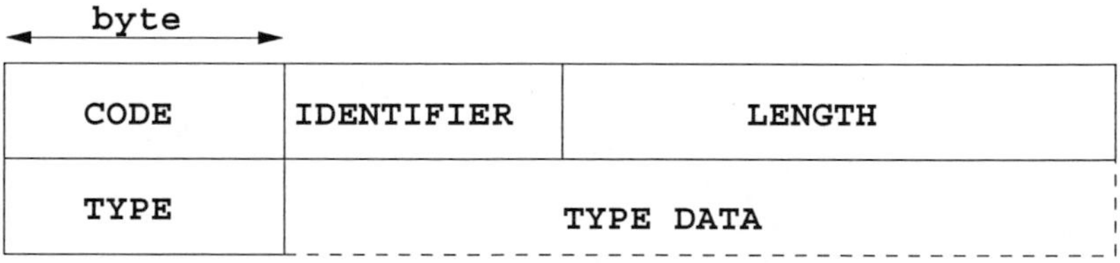

CODE	IDENTIFIER	LENGTH
TYPE	TYPE DATA	

Figure 4.11: EAP Request/Response Packet Format

As mentioned above, a request message carries a code of 1 and a response packet a code of 2. The type field within the request packet is used to determine the value being requested and must be the same in the matching response. Requests are always sent by the authenticator and it is the authenticator that handles retransmissions. If it does not get a response to a request within a certain time, it will retransmit the request with the same identifier as in the first try. In case the response was lost, the peer will see the request for the second time and has to retransmit its original response, whereas in case the request was lost, the peer will process the retransmitted request like a new one. As mentioned above, it is the authenticator that is responsible for the retransmissions, not the back-end authentication server!

If the authenticator is running in pass-through mode, it has to store copies of the requests going through and manage timeout timers, although some methods allow the back-end authentication server to send timeout hints to the authenticator.

Besides the original IETF EAP methods like MD5 (Aboba *et al.*, 2004) and TLS (Simon *et al.*, 2008), there are some vendor specific types like Protected EAP (PEAP) (Palekar *et al.*, 2004), which was developed by Microsoft. Whereas PEAP is a vendor specified EAP method meant for general usage, vendors may also decide to implement and deploy types for some very specific scenarios. These are handled using the expanded EAP type shown in Figure 4.12. The official EAP type for such messages is 254, followed by a 3 byte vendor ID assigned by the IANA. The exact method type is specified in the vendor type field.

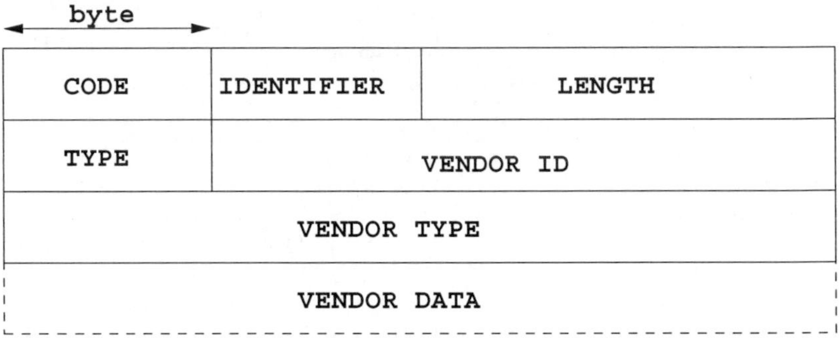

Figure 4.12: EAP Expanded Type

The IETF has a vendor ID of 0 and will use the expanded type to support new general EAP types in case all other 254 type numbers are in use. The initial EAP types specified in (Aboba *et al.*, 2004) are MD5-Challenge, One Time Password (OTP), and Generic Token Card (GTC).

As some EAP methods may require user input, there is a notification type. In addition to a request for user input the notification type may also be used to show the user some information such as a hint that her password is about to expire. EAP methods may forbid the use of notification messages but in case they are allowed and used, they have to be either logged or displayed.

4.2.2   Security Considerations

RFC 3748 (Aboba *et al.*, 2004) defines ten possible attacks on EAP. They range from snooping authentication traffic to man-in-the-middle (MITM) attacks. Snooping the authentication traffic is used to discover user identities since the first identity exchange is usually unsecured. But as several methods exchange another identity later that is different from the first one, just knowing the first identity is usually not a serious problem. Spoofing and modifying packets is more serious but can be avoided using integrity protecting algorithms such as checksums. Furthermore, EAP is vulnerable to Denial of Service (DoS) attacks by spoofing lower layer indications or success and failure packets, replaying EAP packets, or generating packets with overlapping identifiers. One very easy DoS attack is to send the peer a success packet in the right protocol state and dropping the authenticator's failure packet. The peer will try to send ordinary data since it thinks it is allowed to do so but will be blocked by the authenticator. This leads to a DoS on the peer. That kind of DoS is possible since EAP itself does not protect nor authenticate the result indications. EAP methods may choose to do so. However, it will not be possible for an unauthenticated peer to really connect successfully. So this attack is a serious attack for the peer but not for the EAP protected network itself.

Another efficient attack is an offline dictionary attack on the passphrases. This is a serious and potentially successful attack on all passphrase based authentication protocols, not only those running in EAP.

More serious attacks on EAP are MITMs on tunneled methods that do not authenticate the peer. Rogue EAP authenticators may tunnel the EAP traffic to a legitimate server. In case the tunneling protocol is used for key establishment and the rogue authenticator convinces a peer to connect to it and to authenticate successfully to the authentication server, it will be easy for the rogue authenticator to be a MITM in the following data communication since it has got the key from the authentication server. Solutions are either mutual authentication or to require cryptographic binding between the tunneling method and the tunneled method. Another possibility for a MITM is a mutual authentication that actually does two one-way authentications, which is why real mutual authentication is preferred.

Rogue authenticators cannot only establish a MITM, they can also lure a peer into a network he did not plan to connect to, which is known as the "lying provider problem". In order to do so, the authenticator might announce a network he is not connected to and connect the peer to another network. In order to prevent such a lying authenticator, it has been proposed that authentication server and peer compare the information they both got from the authenticator (Clancy & Hoeper, 2009).

Peers that do not accept an EAP authentication method proposed by the authentication server have to reply with a Nak message and propose another method, which may lead to downgrading attacks on EAP methods. Furthermore, an attacker may also either run a downgrading attack on lower layer ciphersuite negotiations or disrupt an EAP negotiation in order to cause the selection of a weak authentication method. Downgrading attacks can be prevented by using only MAC protected Naks. If for whatever reason a weak authentication method has been selected, it might be rather easy for an attacker to take advantage of this and recover the keys if for instance a weak key derivation method has been used.

In case the lower layers do not provide security mechanisms like per-packet integrity, authentication and replay protection, it could happen that a peer uses different authenticators for authentication and data transmission. This allows for an easy deployment of a MITM.

When running EAP over IEEE 802 based lower layers, one has to know that the initial key activation usually only happens after the successful EAP authentication, which means that the first EAP authentication exchange cannot be protected. As the keys are already available for the following re-authentications, these can be protected. Furthermore, it is not possible to authenticate or protect the "link down" message which is another possibility to run a DoS attack on the peer.

Since some implementations allow for limited traffic like account updates if the EAP authentication fails, an attacker may try to tunnel data through this little hole in the authentication process, as it is very popular with DNS at public wireless hotspots (DNS Tunnel, 2009) as described in Section 4.1.

Last but not least it has to be said that it is usually impossible for the peer to decide which authentication server to use as this decision is made by the authenticator. In case the server does not export a server-id, which was not required in pre-RFC 5247 (Aboba *et al.*, 2008) EAP methods, it may not even be possible for the peer to authorize the server.

4.2.3   Transport Layer Security in EAP

EAP-TLS is an EAP method that integrates the Transport Layer Security (TLS) protocol into EAP. It was first published in 1999 as experimental RFC and went into the IETF standards track only in 2008 as RFC 5216 (Simon *et al.*, 2008). TLS as it is defined in (Dierks & Rescorla, 2008) provides mutual authentication, an integrity protected ciphersuite negotiation and a key exchange protocol.

This section starts with an introduction to TLS followed by the details and subtleties when integrating TLS into EAP.

The TLS handshake as specified in (Dierks & Rescorla, 2008) and shown in Figure 4.13 starts with the `client_hello` message including a session ID, a random number and a set of supported ciphersuites and compression algorithms. The session ID is either a new one or an old one describing a session the client wants to resume. It is then up to the server to decide whether it really resumes the session or not. The random number is used for the key derivation algorithm. Furthermore, the `client_hello` includes the client's TLS protocol number. The server answers with the `server_hello` message including the server's TLS protocol number, a random number, the session ID (which is the same as the client's session ID in case session resumption is used), and a set of supported ciphersuites and compression algorithms. In case client and server have disjoint sets of ciphersuites, the TLS handshake will already fail after that message.

Afterwards it is up to the server to send his certificate and to request the client's certificate when using mutual authentication. The `certificate_request` message includes the types of certificates the server accepts (e.g. RSA signing certificate) and may also include a list of certificate authorities (CAs) acceptable to the server. The server finishes its sequence of messages with the `server_hello_done` message.

Assuming mutual authentication, the client will now send its certificate followed by the `client_key_exchange` message which includes the premaster secret. The following `certificate_verify` message is only needed if the client has a signing-only certificate to prove the possession of the private key. As both sides now have everything they need to apply the selected ciphersuite, the client sends `change_cipher_spec` and uses the specified ciphersuite to send the `finished` mes-

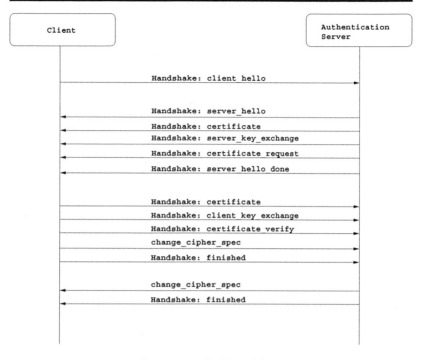

Figure 4.13: TLS Handshake

sage. The server acknowledges the ciphersuite using change_cipher_suite and applies it to its finished message too.

In case the server only possesses a signing certificate that does not contain enough data to allow the client to exchange a premaster secret, the server's certificate message has to be followed by a server_key_exchange message.

As the TLS handshake is vulnerable to downgrading attacks, higher layers should always check whether their security requirements are met prior to sending data via the potentially unsecure channel.

As shown above, like many authentication protocols, TLS usually starts with a message sent by the client, whereas EAP starts with a server message. Therefore a new message had to be included that is sent by the server in order to trigger the TLS authentication on the client side: EAP-Request/EAP-Type=EAP-TLS with a Start Bit S set as shown in Figure 4.14.

The TLS client_hello will then be sent in the peer's response message EAP-Response/EAP-Type=EAP-TLS (TLS client_hello). Every subsequent server message of the TLS handshake is sent as EAP-Request whereas the client/peer

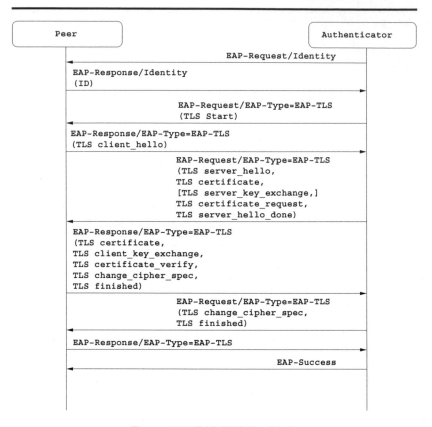

Figure 4.14: EAP TLS Handshake

messages are sent within the EAP-Response messages. The full EAP-TLS authentication is shown in Figure 4.14. The server's certificate message has to include the complete certificate chain since the client is usually offline during the authentication, whereas it should be sufficient for the client to send only its own certificate since the server is usually online and can therefore fetch the rest of the chain for itself.

If the server cannot authenticate the peer for whatever reason, it should send the appropriate TLS alert message and prepare to terminate the conversation. In order to make sure that the client got the alert, the server has to wait for an EAP-Response acknowledging the alert. This response may contain another client_hello which may be accepted by the server and trigger a new TLS handshake. Whether or not a new client_hello is accepted depends on the server implementation, but in order to avoid Denial of Service (DoS) attacks, the server should only allow a limited number of handshake restarts after an unsuccessful peer authentication.

In case the peer cannot authenticate the server, it is not possible to restart the handshake. There is not even the need for the peer to send an alert, this depends on the implementation and may be done in order for the server to log the problem. But if the peer sends an alert it has to wait for the server's request to acknowledge the alert before terminating the conversation.

EAP as specified in (Aboba *et al.*, 2004) allows for a fast re-authentication of the client. This feature is required in a wireless environment in order to ensure that it is still the same client connected to the network. Furthermore, it may be used in case the client has been disconnected only for a short time and wants to reconnect to the network. TLS as defined in (Dierks & Rescorla, 2008) already specifies a session resumption possibility which turned out to be a good way to implement fast re-authentication in EAP-TLS. As in original TLS, it is up to the peer to decide whether it wants to try to resume a session and up to the server to decide whether it accepts this or not, but it has to be mentioned that a peer should never try to resume a session in which it could not authenticate the server.

In contrast to TLS, where it is very likely that a client is always connected to the same server, in an EAP-TLS setup it is likely that the peer has to authenticate to different servers for instance due to the peer's mobility or due to load balancing in the back-end authentication infrastructure. As session resumption over different EAP servers is not supported in EAP-TLS, full handshakes may be required more often than expected.

EAP-TLS supports fragmentation by just setting a More fragments (M) flag in all fragments but the last one, as ordering and loss detection and correction is done on the lower layers of EAP. Every fragment has to be acknowledged by an empty `EAP-Response/EAP-Type=EAP-TLS` respective `EAP-Request/EAP-Type=EAP-TLS`.

Security Considerations

EAP-TLS makes use of certain TLS security features, which makes it a rather secure protocol (the formal proof has been done in (He *et al.*, 2005)). For instance, since TLS makes use of X.509 certificates which include an integrity protected identity it is only natural to use the certificate's subject or subjectAltName fields to determine peer- and server-id instead of using the unprotected identity sent in the first EAP exchange.

Furthermore, using TLS' `hello_request` message, EAP-TLS easily supports privacy: Instead of answering the `certificate_request` with its certificate, the peer sends an empty certificate list which is accepted by a server supporting privacy. The TLS session will be established with server authentication only but the first message inside that session is a `hello_request` sent by the server forcing the client to start a new handshake protected by the active session. The client has to send its certificate during that handshake. If it supplies another empty list, the complete authentication is considered unsuccessful and the server terminates the session. In case the second handshake is completed successfully, it is the second master key that will be used to secure the following data communication.

Aside from the well-known downgrading attacks, attacks on EAP-TLS are mostly DoS attacks. Since the EAP header fields such as the code, ID, and length field are not integrity protected, bad server implementations may be vulnerable to buffer overflow attacks if an attacker adds additional data to a message causing a packet to be longer than the value mentioned in the length field.

Summarizing, one can say that the mutual authentication using X.509 certificates makes EAP-TLS one of the most secure EAP authentication protocols especially when storing the private key in a trusted device.

Problems From the User's Perspective

As mentioned in Section 4.2.3, EAP-TLS is a very secure authentication protocol when using X.509 certificates on both sides. But this requirement also makes the protocol very uncomfortable for normal users since the process of requesting an X.509 certificate is rather complicated and usually requires a lot of user interaction.

Figure 4.15: Certificate Request Form on www.swissdigicert.ch

Figure 4.15 shows the form used by `www.swissdigicert.ch` to allow users to request a new certificate. In order to be able to fill out the form, one must know the meaning of *PEM Encoded PKCS#10 Request*, which may be unknown even to expert users. Most CAs provide their customers with forms like this which makes the process of requesting a new X.509 certificate really uncomfortable.

Furthermore, in order to make the certificate handling really secure, the private key should be stored in a trusted device such as a smart card which normal users usually do not have due to the lack of generally available trusted devices.

EAP-TLS with mutual authentication is therefore so far almost unusable for normal users.

4.2.4 Second Generation Cellular Networks Authentication in EAP

The EAP method for the Global System for Mobile Communications (GSM) Subscriber Identity Modules (SIM) is – as the name suggests – an EAP method making use of SIM credentials. It was originally specified by the 3rd Generation Partnership Project (3GPP) and published as informational RFC in the IETF as information for the Internet community (Haverinen & Salowey, 2006). EAP-SIM makes use of 2G mobile network credentials, whereas EAP-AKA as presented in Section 4.2.5 relies on 3G credentials.

An EAP-SIM peer usually has a permanent identity consisting of the International Mobile Subscriber Identity (IMSI), but in order to provide privacy, the EAP server may assign a temporary identity, or even a fast re-authentication identity, where the latter can only be used for fast re-authentication, as the name suggests.

The original GSM authentication algorithm has been described in Section 2.1.3. EAP-SIM uses the GSM authentication with slight modifications: First of all, instead of using K_C for traffic encryption as is done in GSM, EAP-SIM uses K_C to derive keys only. Furthermore, as K_C is only a 64bit key and therefore rather short for secure encryption, EAP-SIM uses several (two to three) $RAND$ values to create several K_C which are then combined to form stronger keying material.

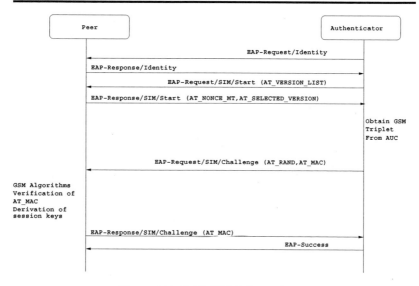

Figure 4.16: EAP-SIM Full Handshake

The full EAP-SIM handshake as shown in Figure 4.16 starts with an EAP-Request
/Identity that is answered by the client with its permanent identity (usually the

International Mobile Subscriber Identity (IMSI)) or a temporary identity assigned by the server in former handshakes. EAP-SIM provides message integrity checks in contrast to EAP itself. As this means that the first identity exchange is not integrity protected, EAP-SIM provides its own identity exchange as shown in Figure 4.17, and it is recommended for the server to run that first and not to rely on the EAP identity.

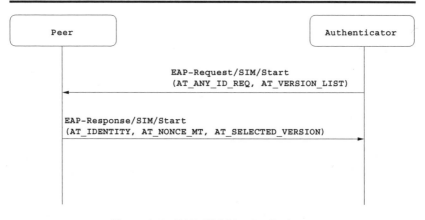

Figure 4.17: EAP-SIM Identity Exchange

The EAP-SIM identity exchange is more flexible than the EAP identity exchange since it allows the server to specify the type of identity it is interested in. Figure 4.17 shows a setup where the server accepts any type of identity – be it a permanent, temporary, or fast re-authentication identity – and therefore sets AT_ANY_ID_REQ in the EAP-Request/SIM/Start message. The client includes its identity into the AT_IDENTITY attribute of EAP-Response/SIM/Start. Instead of setting AT_ANY_IDENTITY_REQ, the server could also set AT_FULLAUTH_ID_REQ, or AT_PERMANENT_ID_REQ. There may be more than one EAP-SIM identity exchange round since the server may refuse an identity of a certain type maybe because he cannot map it to a client. But there cannot be more than three rounds at maximum with AT_ANY_IDENTITY_REQ only acceptable for the peer in the first round and AT_FULLAUTH_ID_REQ not acceptable after AT_PERMANENT_ID_REQ. If the client gets a request for the permanent identity although it has a temporary identity available, it is up to the client to refuse to send the permanent identity and send an error code "unable to process packet" instead. Such a behavior is allowed since it is very likely that a server which has already assigned a temporary identity to a client will only ask for that identity again. Furthermore, if authenticating to another server, it is very likely that different authentication servers of the same network exchange the temporary identities they have assigned. So it may have been an attacker who requested the permanent identity. It is not allowed though to send a temporary identity if the server requested the permanent one. In fact, this will cause the server to give a "general failure" notification.

It has to be mentioned that a pass-through authenticator cannot see the EAP-SIM identity, so the pass-through authenticator will keep the peer under its EAP identity sent in the second message of Figure 4.16.

Aside from the optional identity request, `EAP-Request/SIM/Start` also includes the `AT_VERSION_LIST` containing a list of EAP-SIM versions supported by the server. The peer specifies the version it wants too use in `AT_SELECTED_VERSION`. Furthermore, it sends a `AT_NONCE_MT` that contributes to the key derivation and prevents replay attacks. In order to avoid downgrading attacks on the version, the `AT_VERSION_LIST` and `AT_SELECTED_VERSION` values will be included into the key derivation later in the handshake. After having agreed on a protocol version, it is time to start the GSM challenge-response protocol. But in order to do so, the server needs to request several GSM triplets consisting of $RAND$, K_C, and $SRES$ at the Authentication Center (AUC) of the GSM network. It will usually request two to three triplets at a time, as mentioned above but could request a maximum of five at the same time. The server can store the triplets it does not use immediately for later use bust must never reuse the same values. $RAND$ will be send to the peer within the next `EAP-Request/SIM/Challenge` message, protected by `AT_MAC`. The peer runs the GSM algorithms to calculate $SRES$ and K_C. `AT_MAC` does also include the `AT_NONCE_MT` in order for the client to determine the challenge's freshness. In case the peer cannot verify `AT_MAC`, an error message is sent and the conversation terminates. If `AT_MAC` has been verified correctly, the client calculates another `AT_MAC` over $SRES$ and sends it to the server, which is sufficient for deciding whether the client can be authenticated or not.

The master key MK derived out of a successful full handshake is the SHA-1 signed concatenation of the peer's identity, the n (two to three) obtained K_C, the `NONCE_MT`, the version list, and the selected version.

The Transient EAP (TEKs) and Master Session Keys (MSKs) for link layer security are derived by applying a certain pseudo-random function on MK. There are two TEKs needed: One to calculate `AT_MAC` and one to create `AT_ENCR_DATA` that carries new identities.

Since the EAP-SIM full authentication is rather costly (due to the GSM algorithms running on the client and the request for GSM triplets at the AUC), a fast re-authentication possibility has been defined. If the EAP server has issued a fast re-authentication identity during a former full authentication, the peer may decide to try to do a fast re-authentication. In order to do so, the client answers the `EAP-Request/Identity` (or the EAP-SIM identity `AT_ANY_ID_REQ` shown in Figure 4.17) with its re-authentication identity (see Figure 4.18). If the server accepts the fast re-authentication identity, it sends `AT_IV`, the initialization vector used to encrypt `AT_COUNTER`, `AT_NONCE_S`, and `AT_NEXT_REAUTH_ID`, and `AT_MAC` to protect the message. The `AT_NONCE_S` is used to avoid replay attacks. The client has to verify `AT_MAC` and the freshness of `AT_COUNTER`. The re-authentication counter must be 1 after a full authentication and incremented for every re-authentication. In case the counter does not match the value expected by the peer, the `AT_COUNTER_TOO_SMALL` error is sent including the received counter value. The server can then verify that the

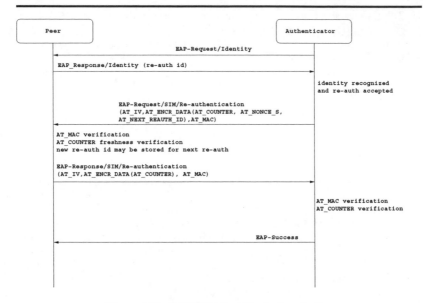

Figure 4.18: EAP-SIM Fast Re-Authentication

peer got the value it sent and trigger a new full authentication. In case the counter could be verified by the peer, it may store the next re-authentication identity and reply with the encrypted counter. The server – like the peer before – verifies AT_MAC and AT_COUNTER and sends the result indication.

EAP-SIM fast re-authentication uses the TEKs derived in the last full handshake, but generates new MSKs and EMSKs every time.

After a certain number of fast re-authentications, a full authentication has to take place.

Security Considerations

EAP-SIM provides a good level of security. It is a lot higher than the GSM security level if the SIM used in EAP-SIM is not used in GSM/GPRS networks! This is due to the fact that the K_C has to be kept secret in EAP-SIM and is used directly for encryption in GSM/GPRS.

In order to prevent replay attacks, EAP-SIM makes use of nonces. Furthermore, EAP-SIM messages are integrity protected and it is even possible to protect the success indication. If a client receives an EAP-Success message at the wrong protocol state, he has to ignore it.

As privacy is only optional in EAP-SIM, it is possible that users always use their permanent identity, which makes them traceable.

Problems From the User's Perspective

Although the SIM is a well-known authentication module for every user, this authentication method requires a SIM slot in every mobile device, rendering it uncomfortable. And even if the user's notebook, for instance, has a SIM slot, the user has to buy a new SIM card used only for WLAN authentication. One reason for this is the security problem with the secrecy of K_C mentioned above, the other reason is that SIMs usually support only single sessions. That means that a user cannot receive or make any calls while authenticating to a network and as re-authentication is required from time to time, she cannot even disconnect her SIM after the first authentication.

Concluding, EAP-SIM is a very secure and therefore preferred authentication method with a mixed user experience.

4.2.5 Third Generation Cellular Networks Authentication in EAP

EAP-AKA is an EAP method for the 3G mobile network authentication called Authentication and Key Agreement (AKA). It has been specified by the 3GPP and – having been checked for compliance with EAP (Aboba *et al.*, 2004) – published as informational RFC (Arkko & Haverinen, 2006) similar to EAP-SIM.

The 3G AKA has some improvements compared to 2G (GSM) AKA, such as much longer keys and mutual authentication.

The 3G or UMTS network knows two different types of identities:

1. The IMSI for the Circuit Switched (CS) radio network, and

2. the Network Address Identifier (NAI) for the Packet Switched (PS) IMS (IP Multimedia Subsystem).

Figure 4.19 shows a successful full authentication between peer and EAP server, which may be running on the authenticator or as back-end authentication server. Like every EAP conversation, EAP-AKA starts with `EAP-Request/Identity`. Since this first message exchange cannot be protected, the authors of (Arkko & Haverinen, 2006) propose to use `EAP-Request/AKA-Identity` instead, which can be protected using the `AT_CHECKCODE` attribute.

Similarly to EAP-SIM, EAP-AKA knows three types of identities: permanent identities, pseudonyms, and fast re-authentication identities. The permanent identity is the one that belongs uniquely to one peer and can be used in full authentication. Pseudonyms and fast re-authentication identities are assigned by the server and can be used for full authentication (pseudonyms) and fast re-authentication (fast re-authentication identities). As already mentioned, the permanent identity is usually the peer's IMSI or a NAI. The generation of the pseudonyms and fast re-authentication identities is highly implementation dependent since only the server that generated them needs to be able to map them to permanent identities according to (Arkko & Haverinen, 2006). However, in order to support mobility, there should be a pseudonym exchange between all the EAP servers of the peer's home network. In case there is no such exchange or something went wrong, a new server has to request the permanent identity. Since fast re-authentication requires the same server

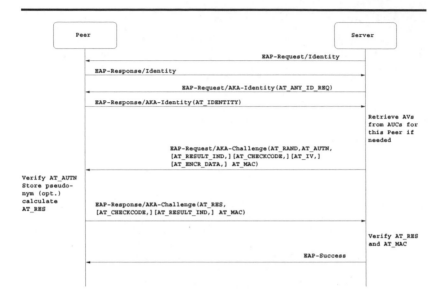

Figure 4.19: EAP-AKA Full Authentication

in order to reuse a session context, the fast re-authentication identity may include a realm name to ensure correct routing. Furthermore, it should include a random number to associate it with a full authentication context and render it unpredictable.

Like in EAP-SIM, there can be three identity rounds at the maximum:

1. The server asks for `AT_ANY_ID_REQ` (as shown in Figure 4.19), gets a fast re-authentication identity and cannot or does not want to map that identity to an old session.

2. The server may now ask for `AT_FULLAUTH_ID_REQ` and get a pseudonym that it cannot map to a permanent identity.

3. Last of all, the server may ask for `AT_PERMANENT_ID_REQ`.

It is obviously also possible to ask directly for `AT_FULLAUTH_ID_REQ` or `AT_PERMA-NENT_ID_REQ`.

In case `EAP-Request/AKA-Identity` - `EAP-Response/AKA-Identity` is used to send the peer's identity, a possible pass-through authenticator will not be able to read the identity and will therefore use the identity sent in `EAP-Response/Identity` to identify a conversation.

After having received an acceptable pseudonym or permanent identity, the server has to check whether it still has unused authentication vectors $AV(1..n)$ for that peer. If not, it requests new ones at the peer's Home Location Register (HLR).

`EAP-Request/AKA-Challenge` includes the $AT\_RAND(i)$ and $AT\_AUTN(i)$ needed for the AKA protocol. Furthermore, it includes `AT_MAC` which covers the complete EAP packet and may include `AT_RESULT_IND` in order to request protected result indications, `AT_CHECKCODE`, which allows for a simple integrity protection without the need for keys, `AT_IV`, which is the initialization vector for `AT_ENCR_DATA` that may carry a new pseudonym or fast re-authentication identity.

It is then up to the peer to run the AKA algorithms in order to verify $AT\_AUTN(i)$ and to calculate $AT\_RES(i)$. Furthermore, if the peer supports pseudonyms and fast re-authentication identities and `AT_ENCR_DATA` is included, it stores the new identity.

`EAP-Response/AKA-Challenge` includes $AT\_RES(i)$, as well as `AT_MAC` (again covering the complete packet) as well as the optional `AT_CHECKCODE` and `AT_RESULT_IND`. This message is also the implicit indication that the peer was able to authenticate the server successfully. If the server is then able to authenticate the peer too by verifying $AT\_RES(i)$ and `AT_MAC`, the conversation ends with `EAP-Success`.

The master key MK is derived as $MK = SHA1(Identity|IK(i)|CK(i))$ where $Identity$ is either the EAP identity or the value of `AT_IDENTITY` and $IK(i)$ and $CK(i)$ parameters of the authentication vector $AV(i)$ as discussed in Section 2.2.3. The MSK, $EMSK$, and TEKs are calculated by applying a pseudo random function on MK.

Like in EAP-SIM, there are two TEKs defined for EAP-AKA itself: K_{aut} and K_{encr}, which are needed to calculate `AT_MAC` and `AT_ENCR_DATA`.

EAP-AKA is easily extensible by defining new attributes but one has to take care of the fact that the EAP-AKA does not support fragmentation!

When using fast re-authentication, a counter `AT_COUNTER` is used to avoid replay attacks and limit the number of fast re-authentications between two full authentications.

Security Considerations

As already mentioned above, it may happen that a peer receives a request for its permanent identity although it still has a valid pseudonym. Since there may have been an attacker who injected that request, it is up to the peer to send his permanent identity now or to terminate the conversation. A liberal peer may assume that the network can loose pseudonyms whereas a conservative peer may assume that the network is able to hold them and refuse to answer the request.

Since attackers may also forge error packets, EAP-AKA implementations should never rely on correct error reporting.

Furthermore, a peer should only accept `EAP-Success` at the correct protocol state and `EAP-Failure` if there was a notification round that reported an error or if it detected an error itself. In order to protect the results, the server should request `AT_RESULT_IND`.

In general, EAP-AKA supports identity privacy if pseudonyms are used and mutual authentication with an effective key strength of 128bit. In order to protect integrity and confidentiality and to protect against replay attacks, EAP-AKA defines the `AT_MAC`, `AT_IV`, `AT_ENCR_DATA`, and `AT_COUNTER` attributes that have been explained in this section. As AT_MAC already requires keys that are not available in the beginning, there is another integrity protection attribute that can be calculated without keys: AT_CHECKCODE. Since EAP-Response/Nak is not protected, EAP-AKA is vulnerable to downgrading attacks.

Lastly, it has to be mentioned that it is possible to launch a DoS attack on the 3G back-end infrastructure by sending a huge amount of peer requests that causes the EAP server to flood the AUC. In order to prevent such attacks, the server should limit the number of requests sent to the AUC.

4.2.6   Interim Conclusion

Out of the authentication methods above, the ones used in public wireless networks are captive portals and EAP-SIM. Captive portals are easy to deploy and use whereas EAP-SIM provides the level of security needed for a reliable network operation. However, EAP-SIM comes with the disadvantages described in Section 4.2.4, which is why this thesis concentrates on finding a new authentication protocol that is based on another piece of trusted hardware - the Trusted Platform Module (TPM).

4.3   Authentication, Authorization, and Accounting

As already mentioned, AAA is short for authentication, authorization, and accounting and describes protocols running between the authenticator and the authentication server. The AAA protocol that is used most widely today is probably RADIUS although it already has a successor called DIAMETER. This section discusses both protocols in detail.

────────────────────── **Notations** ──────────────────────

The notation used in this sections differs a bit from the notation used before. The **client** in an Authentication, Authorization, and Accounting (AAA) infrastructure is the RADIUS client, in other words, the client is the network access server (NAS) (that is the authenticator), whereas the **user** is the entity that wants to be authenticated to the network. Lastly, the **server** is the authentication server, also called the **AAA server**.

4.3.1   The RADIUS Protocol

The Remote Authentication Dial In User Service (RADIUS) protocol is a transaction based application layer protocol for carrying authentication, authorization, and configuration information between a network access server and an authentication server (Rigney *et al.*, 2000). RADIUS also provides an extension for accounting (Rigney, 2000).

Figure 4.20 shows the architecture of a network making use of the RADIUS protocol. The user on the left side is the entity that wants to get access to a network or a service. When trying to connect to it, it starts at the network access server (NAS), which checks whether the user is already authenticated or not. In case the user is not yet authenticated, the NAS asks the authentication server to authenticate

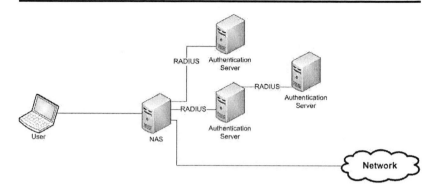

Figure 4.20: Network Authentication Architecture Using RADIUS

the user using the RADIUS protocol. The authentication server may ask another authentication server if needed, again using the RADIUS protocol. Furthermore, there may be several authentication servers managing the same user in order to enable load balancing and redundancy. After having authenticated the user, she gets access to the network or service using the NAS as entry point.

RADIUS was developed to provide a standardized dial-in infrastructure for the University of Michigan in the early 1990s (Vollbrecht, 2006) and still is the standard network authentication solution today. It was standardized by the IETF in 1997 and updated in 2000 (Rigney *et al.*, 2000). Even today, there is still an IETF working group discussing new RADIUS extensions.

RADIUS was a rather simple protocol at the beginning, consisting mainly of four messages: `access-request`, `access-challenge`, `access-accept`, and `access-reject`. In order to ensure security between the NAS and the authentication server, RADIUS makes use of shared secrets that are never transmitted over the network.

Figure 4.21 shows the format for `access-request`. This message is sent by the NAS to the authentication server if a user wants to get access to the network. The NAS will usually ask the user for an identity of the format username@realm and a password and transmit them to the authentication server using this message. The code is 1 and the identifier is unique for each set of attribute values. Length determines the length of the message and parameters like username and password are transmitted as attributes. The values of username and password depend on the actual authentication protocol used. The request authenticator field carries a 16 byte random number used to avoid replay attacks. Furthermore, the request authenticator value is used to encrypt the password in order to avoid transmitting clear-text passwords. The password encryption works as follows: the request authenticator value appended to the shared secret is MD5 hashed and the resulting 16 byte digest value XORed with the password. The resulting value is then transmitted to the authentication server. Besides transmitting username and password, the NAS also

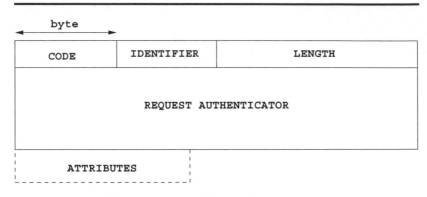

Figure 4.21: RADIUS Access-Request Message

transmits a NAS ID to identify itself and the port ID or number the user is accessing. Further, an `access-request` may include more information about the service the user wants to access, e.g. the host the user wants to connect to. For more options see (Rigney *et al.*, 2000).

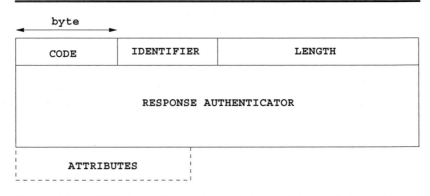

Figure 4.22: RADIUS Access-Accept, Access-Reject, and Access-Challenge Message

Before processing the `access-request`, the server has to validate the NAS and check whether it has the appropriate shared secret. In case the server does not have a shared secret for that client, the `access-request` must be discarded. If the authentication server is able to make its decision based on the attributes sent in `access-request`, it sends either `access-accept` or `access-reject`. The format, which is the same for both messages, is shown in Figure 4.22. The code for `access-accept` is 2, and 3 for `access-reject`. The identifier value has to be the same as in the `access-request` related to this response in order for the NAS to be able to match response and request. The response authenticator is a concatenation over the code, identifier, and length value, plus the request authenticator, the attributes and the shared secret. `access-accept` messages may include configuration (authorization) attributes like the IP address to be assigned to the user, or the maximum period of time the user is allowed to access the requested service or network. The `access-reject` message may contain a displayable text attribute informing the user about the reason for rejecting him.

In case the information sent in `access-request` was not sufficient to authenticate the user, the authentication server sends `access-challenge`. This message has the same format like `access-accept` and `access-reject` but carries a code of 11. The challenge to be sent to the user is included in the attributes and usually consists of an unpredictable random number that has to be displayed to the user by the NAS. The user will then type this challenge into a dedicated device and send the response to the NAS. The NAS includes the response into a new `access-request` message with a new identifier and the user's password replaced by the response. It is then up to the authentication server, whether it can already decide whether to authenticate the user or not or whether it needs more information resulting in another `access-challenge`.

Furthermore, `access-challenge` may include a timeout attribute to disable brute-force and replay attacks.

As it is not mandatory for a NAS to implement the RADIUS challenge-response mechanism, it might be possible that a NAS treats `access-challenge` as `access-reject`.

An authentication server may also act as proxy server, for instance for roaming users. If an `access-request` arrives for a roaming user, the authentication server will take the role of a RADIUS client and forward the request to the appropriate authentication server that holds the user's record. The decision which authentication server is responsible for which user is usually made based on the user's realm. As the shared secrets always protect a link between RADIUS client and server, a proxy server has to decrypt the incoming messages and re-encrypt them with the shared secret for the following link.

As already mentioned, RADIUS does not only provide authentication and authorization, but also accounting as specified in (Rigney, 2000). If accounting is used for a certain user, the NAS sends an `accounting-request` of the format shown in Figure 4.21 including the user's IP and the `accounting-start` attribute. The server acknowledges the receipt of the request and the start of the accounting with `accounting-response`. In order to stop the accounting, the NAS sends `accounting-request` with the `accounting-stop` attribute and the user's IP, which has to be acknowledged again. For a more detailed description of RADIUS accounting see (Rigney, 2000).

Although work has already been done to run RADIUS over TCP (DeKok, 2009b), the protocol as specified in (Rigney *et al.*, 2000) runs over UDP. The original reason for that choice were the special timing constraints of RADIUS as well as its statelessness. A user is willing to wait several seconds for authentication, which means an aggressive retransmission behavior is not needed, RADIUS retransmission timers are sufficient. But a user might not be willing to wait several minutes, which may be the time TCP needs to deliver all the packets to the chosen authentication server. RADIUS as it is will use another authentication server if the original server does not reply after a certain number of retransmissions. Furthermore, the authors of (Rigney *et al.*, 2000) assume that servers come and go, can be rebooted etc. Using TCP needs a costly detection of lost connections here, whereas UDP allows to switch servers faster.

RADIUS does not provide any keep-alive mechanism, since such messages could cause serious load problems on the server (as discussed in (Rigney *et al.*, 2000), RADIUS already has scaling and congestion problems). Instead, the authors of (Rigney *et al.*, 2000) propose to do the keep-alive implicitly using the `access-request` (if there is no reply after a certain number of retransmissions, the server is probably dead), or to use the Simple Network Management Protocol (SNMP) for that purpose.

Although RADIUS was a simple protocol in the beginning, common implementations often extend the protocol in a non-standard manner making interoperability hard (Mitton, 2000) (Nelson & DeKok, 2007).

RADIUS EAP Support

RADIUS support for the Extensible Authentication Protocol (EAP) explained in Section 4.2 has been standardized in 2003 (Aboba & Calhoun, 2003). Two new attributes have been defined in order to support EAP: `EAP-Message` and `Message-Authenticator`. `EAP-Message` carries the EAP message itself, whereas `Message-Authenticator` contains an HMAC-MD5 digest over the EAP type, identifier, length, the RADIUS request authenticator and attributes in order to protect the message. This digest is needed in order to avoid attacks on EAP on the RADIUS part.

If a user tries to connect to a NAS using EAP, the NAS will send an `access-request` message including the EAP message to the server. The EAP conversation will then run over `access-challenge`, `access-request` exchanges. In case the server does not support EAP, an `access-reject` will be sent immediately. The end of the EAP conversation is signaled by an `access-accept` including EAP Success or `access-reject` including EAP Failure.

The NAS should try to determine the user's identity either by sending `EAP-Request/Identity` itself or by other means in order to include the user identity in the `access-request` message, so that non-EAP servers are supported as well. In case the NAS cannot determine the user's identity, it can send an `access-request` to indicate EAP start which triggers the server to send `EAP Request/Identity` inside the next `access-challenge`. If the NAS has included a user identity in the first `access-request`, this identity has to be included in every following message in order for the NAS to be able to keep track of the conversation based on the identity.

For every passing EAP message, the NAS has to check the *code*, *identifier* and *length* fields. Furthermore, as the server cannot determine the MTU by himself, the NAS can provide MTU information to the server using the `Framed-MTU` attribute of `access-request`.

Security in RADIUS/EAP should be enabled using IPSec with IKE for key management and IPSec EPS for the per-packet confidentiality, authentication, integrity, and replay protection.

4.3.2 The DIAMETER Protocol

DIAMETER (Calhoun *et al.*, 2003) is the successor of RADIUS and according to the name "twice as good as RADIUS". Like RADIUS, DIAMETER is an authentication, authorization, and accounting (AAA) protocol. It tries to include the new requirements for AAA protocols that have evolved over time such as failover mechanisms, transmission level security, reliable transport, agent support, support for server initiated requests, and auditability.

RADIUS did not define any failover mechanisms, but as they are needed under certain circumstances, vendors have implemented them, making failover implementation dependent. The same applies to the transmission level security since RADIUS does not require security on the transport layer, only on the application layer – in contrast to DIAMETER, which requires IPSec and allows optionally for TLS. RFC 3588 (Calhoun *et al.*, 2003) suggests using IPSec for the network's edges and intra-domain traffic and TLS for inter-domain traffic. IPSec and TLS are sufficient for environments with no untrusted third party agent. If this constraint is violated, end-to-end security algorithms should be used. In order to provide per-packet authentication, integrity protection, and confidentiality, the IPSec Encapsulation Security Payload (ESP) protocol should be used. Furthermore, the Internet Key Exchange (IKE) protocol should be used for node authentication, SA negotiation, and key management. Node authentication must be supported using shared keys and may be supported with certificates. In case TLS is used, mutual authentication is mandatory. It has to be noted that a node should always use the same security protocol for every connection (that is either IPSec or TLS) in order to avoid redundancy or – worse – vulnerabilities arising from an heterogeneous setup.

Furthermore, although there have already been discussions about running RADIUS over TCP (DeKok, 2009b), the original standard (Rigney *et al.*, 2000) requires UDP to be used with RADIUS. As UDP is an unreliable protocol, dealing with packet loss is left to the particular RADIUS implementation. Additionally, it may be asked whether accounting via unreliable connections is a good idea. DIAMETER overcomes that problem by requiring the Stream Control Transmission Protocol (SCTP) or TCP. A client must support either TCP or SCTP, whereas servers and agents have to support both. If a clients supports both, a conversation should always start with SCTP.

Furthermore, the new protocol provides a so called agent support. Agents are nodes with a proxy-, redirect-, relay-, or translation functionality. Proxies do not only forward requests but are also allowed to evaluate requests against local policies and to reject messages. Relay agents do not evaluate messages against policies, they are used for routing purposes. It is usually enough for a DIAMETER client to know a relay agent to route packets to, who will then take care of forwarding the message to an appropriate server. Otherwise, the client has to know all servers, which leads to scalability problems. In contrast to a relay agent, a redirect agent does not forward messages to servers the client does not know, but instead refers the client to a server to allow them to communicate directly. Last but not least, a translation agent translates RADIUS messages into DIAMETER messages and vice versa. The translation agents are the only possibility to use RADIUS and DIAMETER within the same network as DIAMETER does not provide any backwards compatibility. It has to be mentioned that a DIAMETER node may be an agent and a server at the same time.

In contrast to RADIUS where messages are always initiated by the client, DIAMETER allows for server initiated messages, making user disconnects and re-authentication possible. There is also an optional auditability option in order to make the protocol more suitable for commercial deployment. Auditability together with the reliability mentioned above makes DIAMETER more suitable for large scale roaming. Another feature allowing for more scalability is the dynamic client discovery and configuration option where RADIUS required manual configuration. Dynamic client discovery can be done using the Service Location Protocol (SLP) v2 (Guttman *et al.*, 1999), the Naming Authority Pointer (NAPTR) (Mealling & Daniel, 2000), or DNS. Of course it is still allowed to configure new clients manually. Lastly, DIAMETER supports capability negotiation, error handling and mandatory and optional attribute value pairs (AVP).

As in RADIUS, all data is delivered using AVPs, with some being defined by the base protocol itself and others by so called applications.

The DIAMETER base protocol as defined in (Calhoun *et al.*, 2003) can be used for accounting as it is but has to be extended for every application making use of authentication and authorization. There are two applications already mentioned in (Calhoun *et al.*, 2003):

1. a DIAMETER application for Mobile IPv4 (Calhoun *et al.*, 2005a), and

2. a DIAMETER application for NAS environments (Calhoun *et al.*, 2005b).

A node that wants to be a DIAMETER client has to support all applications, otherwise it has to be called DIAMETER <application name> client. The same applies to servers and proxies. It does obviously not apply to relays and redirects since those are transparent to the application. The DIAMETER base protocol is "only" about capability negotiation, about the sending of messages and about how peers may be abandoned.

If a client wants to start a DIAMETER conversation, it sends a message to another node with the application specific AVP set. The only fixed AVP that has to be sent also is the session ID that references the current session. This ID will be used in every following message to identify the session. Furthermore, messages contain the application's ID in order to enable relay and proxy agents to look for a server that supports the application. In case no such server exists or the agents cannot find such a server, a `DIAMETER_UNABLE_TO_DELIVER` message is sent back. In general, application IDs are advertised during capability negotiation.

The capability negotiation phase also includes the advertising of the supported accounting applications in order to avoid the acceptance of unbillable services.

In order to ensure end-to-end security, all paths between two nodes have to be authenticated and authorized. This is especially important for accounting. A node that seems to be suspect for whatever reason will not receive any messages anymore. In order to exclude this node, a failover algorithm takes place that reconfigures the routes. If the node becomes trustworthy again, it may be included into the routing again.

DIAMETER is extensible through the addition of new commands and AVPs.

DIAMETER/EAP Application

In 2005, DIAMETER has been extended by an EAP application (Eronen *et al.*, 2005) comparable to RADIUS' EAP extension. The DIAMETER/EAP application is based on the Network Access Server Requirements (NASREQ) (Calhoun *et al.*, 2005b). The network access server (NAS) is usually playing the role of an EAP pass-through authenticator, whereas the DIAMETER server is the EAP back-end authentication server.

Like every new application, DIAMETER/EAP defines some new commands and attribute value pairs (AVPs). Furthermore, (Eronen *et al.*, 2005) defines how RADIUS/EAP and DIAMETER/EAP can work together, which is beyond the scope of this thesis.

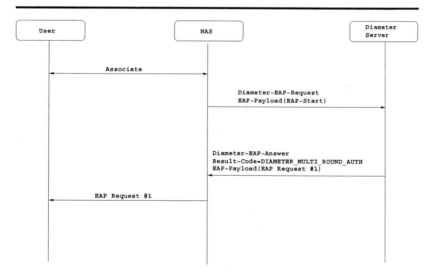

Figure 4.23: Start of a DIAMETER/EAP Conversation

Figure 4.23 shows the start of a DIAMETER/EAP conversation. It starts with the user associating with the NAS, which is most likely an access point in the context of public wireless networks. The NAS will then trigger the EAP message exchange with the server by sending a `Diameter-EAP-Request/EAP-Payload(EAP-Start)`. The server answers with `Diameter-EAP-Answer/ Result-Code=DIAMETER_MULTI_ROUND_AUTH/ EAP-Payload(EAP Request #1)` usually including the identity request. The NAS forwards the EAP request to the user. Alternatively it may be the NAS sending the identity request. The identity sent by the user then has to be used in every subsequent user-name AVP.

The conversation goes on until the server sends `Diameter-EAP-Answer` with a result-code AVP of either `DIAMETER_SUCCESS` or `DIAMETER_FAILURE`. If the result code indicates success and authorization has been requested for that user, the server could also include the authorization AVPs, although authorization can also be done separately. Furthermore, a success message may also include the EAP MSK, which raises a privacy issue since the message is readable by agents in-between. IPSec and TLS only guarantee hop-by-hop protection and no end-to-end security. A network setup with a direct connection between NAS and DIAMETER server is therefore obviously more secure than a setup consisting of agents other than redirect agents between these two parties.

As even redirect agents may be compromised and redirect a request to a malicious server, DIAMETER client and server should always check whether their counterpart is authorized to play his role. However, there are serious threats by attackers who manage to compromise an authorized agent, ranging from allowing unauthorized users and blocking authorized users to sending commands to the NAS to call expensive numbers.

As in every EAP setup, it is up to the pass-through authenticator to validate the EAP header. Furthermore the NAS – the pass-though authenticator in this setup – may send a MTU hint to the server using the framed-MTU AVP analogously to RADIUS. In order to avoid Denial of Service (DoS) attacks on the NAS, it should only accept a certain number of invalid packets from the same user.

As already mentioned above, DIAMETER/EAP defines new commands and AVPs. The new commands are `Diameter-EAP-Request` and `Diameter-EAP-Answer` whose use is illustrated in Figure 4.23. The AVPs include the `EAP-Payload` AVP shown in Figure 4.23, the `EAP-Reissued-Payload` AVP sent by the server in case a non-fatal error occurred due to an invalid EAP response, the `EAP-Master-Session-Key` AVP to carry the MSK, the `EAP-Key-Name` AVP to carry the MSK's name, and the `Accounting-EAP-Auth-Method` AVP to realize accounting in DIAMETER/EAP.

EAP re-authentication may be requested by the server by issueing re-authentication requests, which is directly supported in DIAMETER.

4.3.3   Interim Conclusion

Authentication, authorization, and accounting protocols like RADIUS and DIAMETER are needed in the back-end of a public (wireless) network infrastructure. They will be used unchanged in the context of this thesis since they do not care for the EAP method used to authenticate a peer.

5

Trusted Computing

The Trusted Computing Group (TCG) has been formed in 2003 as a successor of the Trusted Computing Platform Alliance (TCPA) that started work in 1999. It is an industrial consortium that is aimed at designing a specification for platforms that act as a foundation for trust for software processes. This goal is a result of the observation that there are secure and trusted operating systems for servers but there is no ubiquitous solution for clients. There are some very complicated proprietary solutions that are deployed in business networks, but there is nothing similar for home networks. This might not be an issue for private computers since they usually carry less sensitive data (as long as you do not use them for online banking of course), but it is an issue for business systems. As more and more people use their business computers for private purposes as well (and vice versa), trust becomes an issue again.

Nowadays, the TCG includes more than 150 companies with big players like Microsoft, HP, IBM, Intel, and RSA Security. At the time of writing this thesis, the TCG consists of 11 working groups dealing with different aspects like the Trusted Platform Module (TPM), Authentication Infrastructures, Mobile Clients, and virtualization aspects.

This chapter starts with a short introduction to concepts like trust, security and privacy, goes on with a more detailed explanation of the TCG standards and ends with a detailed description of the TPM as well as some TPM applications.

5.1 Trust, Privacy, and Security Concepts

What is trust? Trust is hard to specify in technical terms. Colloquially spoken, trust is "a firm belief in the reliability or truth or strength, etc., of a person or thing" (Balacheff *et al.*, 2003). Obviously, such a belief makes the believer vulnerable to attacks by the trusted object/person. Furthermore, trust is dynamic. It is hard to build and easy to lose. This colloquial description has been translated into a technical one by the TCPA: "A trusted component, operation, or process is one whose behavior is predictable under almost any operating condition and which is highly resistant to subversion by application software, viruses, and a given level of physical interference." (Balacheff *et al.*, 2003). The common software solutions that

were designed to prove the trustworthiness of a system fail to fulfill even the first
requirement ("highly resistant to subversion by application software"). This makes
applications like network endpoint assessment really hard.

Besides the concept of trust, there are the concepts of security and privacy.
Security means that data cannot be tampered with, whereas privacy requires authentication in case some only the owner of information is allowed to read and use
it. (Balacheff *et al.*, 2003) even distinguishes between privacy and secrecy. Private
information belongs to a person and cannot be used by other people. Secret information is never known by anybody else. A credit card number for instance is private
but not secret.

The next sections deal with the standards and concepts published by the Trusted
Computing Group.

5.2   Features of Trusted Computing

The Trusted Computing Group (TCG) specifies a lot of features of trusted computing such as so-called enhanced signatures, where an entity does not only sign data
but does also include data about its platform's integrity. This allows a verifier to
really judge the value of the signature. In today's software-only solutions, a tampered platform could still produce valid signatures, and nobody can verify whether
the platform (and therefore its signature) is trustworthy.

In order to make sure that a platform is really trustworthy, one has to start by
verifying its state right from the beginning, which means right from the first boot
steps. There are two possibilities for doing that. The first possibility is called *secure
boot* and will cause an exception in case something is not as expected. This may
render a platform unusable until the problem has been fixed. The other possibility
called *trusted or authenticated boot* allows a platform to boot to any state, but
reports everything. In case the platform connects to a network, it can be identified
and checked for correctness by asking for these reports. So it is pretty easy for
the network to determine a device's trustworthiness. But what about the user? In
order for the user to be really sure about the trust state of her platform, she needs to
challenge it, for instance using a computing device such as a smart card. Since this is
rather uncomfortable, it is also possible to bind a user picture to a trusted platform
state, which is only released and shown if the platform has booted into a trusted
state. In order to avoid replay attacks, the picture might include a time stamp or
there might be several pictures. The latter is the more user-friendly solution, which
has to be prioritized since users should never have to decide between ease of use
and security. This is especially important since users today are used to insecure
platforms and do not care. So in order to get people used to trusted platforms,
there must be good and simple usage scenarios.

The process of binding data like the picture mentioned above is a new form of
privacy protection that has been introduced by the TCPA: a secret is not revealed
if the platform is not in an approved state.

Since software-only solutions are not sufficient to provide the desired features, the
TCPA has started to specify a hardware module called Trusted Platform Module

(TPM), which acts as trusted component in every general platform. In order to promote the dissemination of the TPM, it has to be a cheap module that provides only those function that *must* be trusted and allow the module to act as a root of trust.

If a platform is trusted, it is well suited to providing a protected storage for secrets, which is a desirable feature. But on the other hand, one of the main problems of trusted platforms is that they have to deal with import/ export regulations. This is one of the reasons why the TCG reduces their trusted part (the Trusted Platform Module (TPM)) to the most minimal set of functions needed to make a platform trustworthy.

The operating system running on a trusted platform has to be TCG compatible, which means that it has to be able to detect security critical changes being made and to decide which events have to be recorded.

The next section deals with the properties and features of the Trusted Platform Module in more detail.

5.3 The Trusted Platform Module (TPM)

In order to make every platform a trusted platform, the TCG specified a small piece of hardware that will be/ is included into almost every new computer and takes the role of a root of trust. This small piece of hardware is called Trusted Platform Module (TPM) and currently specified in (TCG, 2007b), (TCG, 2006a), and (TCG, 2006b). In order to circumvent import/ export regulations and in order to keep the module cheap, the TPM does only provide functionality that must be realized in hardware to make it trusted. This functionality includes hashing – so far SHA-1 –, a random number generator (RNG), asymmetric key generation – so far RSA –, and asymmetric encryption and decryption – so far RSA. Symmetric encryption algorithms like 3DES have to be implemented in software, but the appropriate keys may be stored inside the TPM. The reason why the TPM does not provide symmetric encryption itself is that symmetric encryption requires a much better performance than can be provided by such a cheap module.

The TPM supports different types of authorization for commands send from the TSS discussed in Section 5.3.1, two that can be used to authenticate locally or remotely and one that needs physical presence. The two protocols that can be used remotely as well as locally are called OSAP and OIAP. Both allow to exchange nonces in a challenge-response manner. OSAP is short for Object Specific Authorization Protocol and allows to access the same object several times by generating a temporary secret that is used internally for subsequent accesses. This protocol is mandatory for setting and resetting usage authorization data. On the other hand, there is the Object Independent Authorization Protocol (OIAP) that can be used to access multiple objects by creating multiple authorization sessions internally. Last of all, there are some commands that are so critical that they require physical presence. Physical presence is usually indicated by a key stroke (for instance one of the Fn keys on Lenovo notebooks) and required for commands like resetting the module. Furthermore, physical presence is used if cryptographical authorization cannot be used, for instance if there are not enough resources on the platform, as it is the case before the operating system is loaded. Enabling the TPM is the only command that must use physical presence under all circumstances.

As a side remark, one has to mention that the TCG chose to require a length of 20 bytes for every authorization secret. It does not matter whether the secret itself is 20 bytes long or whether the secret has been hashed into a 20 bytes hash like SHA-1.

Furthermore, even if it is possible to create objects without assigning authorization data, one should always assign some, since the authorization is also used as implicit checksum on data exchanged with the TPM. Using a NULL secret makes the checksum predictable.

In order to use a TPM, the module has to be owned first, which is done using the `takeOwnership` command. It is then up to the entity or person that owns the module whether it uses the module exclusively or whether it allows other people to generate and use some keys too. As the concept of users on a TPM is a bit special, it will be explained more detailedly in the next paragraph.

The owner of a TPM is the one who usually holds the authorization secret for the Storage Root Key (SRK), which is the root key of the key hierarchy in the module. If another user wants to create a new key beneath that root key, the owner respectively SRK authorization secret is needed to create that key. In order to use the key it is then sufficient to know the key's usage secret, which also means that the owner cannot use keys he does not know the usage secret for! It follows that there is no super-user on a TPM. It is even possible for a non-owner to reset the module, since resetting "only" requires physical presence, no authorization secrets. Doing a reset could be seen as a denial of service against the owner, but it is never possible to hijack a TPM owned by somebody else.

Some of the keys stored inside the TPM can be copied to other platforms and TPMs, whereas others have to remain where they originate. The process of copying secrets between TPMs is called migration and described below in a separate section.

Besides providing the secure functions mentioned above (random number generation, RSA encryption and decryption), a TPM can also be used to wrap and unwrap secrets. Those secrets may be for instance RSA or symmetric keys. It is even possible to bind those secrets to a certain platform state – that is to some values of PCRs – in order to be sure a tampered platform cannot misuse or steal them.

Since it is very likely that there will be updates of the TPM specification, it might make sense to allow to upgrade the TPM in situ as well. However, updating will not be an easy process. One has to make sure that an upgrade comes from the manufacturer itself and that it was really meant for that specific TPM. Otherwise attacks on the modules will be very easy. As this is a very complicated process it would be up to the manufacturer to support updates or not.

In order to be sure that a trusted platform including a TPM can really be trusted, there are several entities vouching for the trustworthiness. First of all there is the Trusted Platform Module Entity (TPME) that vouches for a TPM being genuine. The voucher comes in the form of the endorsement credential and it is obvious that it is most likely the manufacturer who takes the role of the TPME. The endorsement credential consists of

1. the statement that it is an endorsement credential,

2. the public endorsement key that has to be injected or generated inside the TPM at the manufacturer's,

3. the specific type of the TPM as well as its security properties, and

4. the reference to the signing TPME.

Furthermore, there is a so-called Validation Entity (VE) that vouches for one or more parts of the platform associated with the Trusted Software Stack (TSS) discussed in Section 5.3.1. It certifies the values of the integrity measurements. The VE may be the component supplier. Third, there is the so called Conformance Entity (CE) – usually a conformance laboratory – that vouches for the TPM as well as the way the platform incorporates the TPM meeting the TCG specifications. The TCG defined two Common Criteria (CC) Protection Profiles (PPs), one for the TPM itself and another one for the attachment of the TPM to the platform and the platform's properties that must be met in order to pass the conformance test.

Then there is a Platform Entity (PE) – probably again the manufacturer – that vouches for a platform containing a specific TPM, which means the PE signs the platform credential, which consists of

1. the statement that it is a platform credential,

2. the reference to the endorsement credential,

3. the reference to the conformance credential,

4. the specific type of the platform and its security properties, as well as of

5. the reference to the signing PE.

Concluding, one can say that an endorsement credential makes a chip a TPM, and a platform credential makes a platform a trusted platform.

5.3.1 Programming (With) The TPM

The TPM is a standard character device that accepts byte streams as specified in (TCG, 2006b). As this programming interface is rather uncomfortable for application programmers, the TCG Software Stack (TSS) has been introduced that is specified in (TCG, 2007a). The two most popular open source implementations of the TSS are TrouSerS (TrouSerS, 2009) and jTSS (TU Graz, 2009), which will be discussed in this section.

Figure 5.1 shows the components of the TSS, which consists of the TPM Device Driver Library (TDDL), the TCG Core Services (TCS), and the TCG Service Provider (TSP). The TDDL represents an API to interface the TPM device driver and therefore provides functionality to opening, closing, sending, and receiving data blobs, querying the device driver's properties and cancelling submitted commands. The TCS manages the TPM resources like authorization sessions and key contexts. Furthermore, it allows for command blob generation and synchronizes application access from the TSP. The TCS can be seen as a software abstraction of the TPM that queues and optimizes the order of TPM commands. Finally, it is the TSP that is called by applications that want to communicate with the TPM. TSPs may run locally or remotely. The TSS has been designed so that local and remote TSPs are handled similarly from a security point of view.

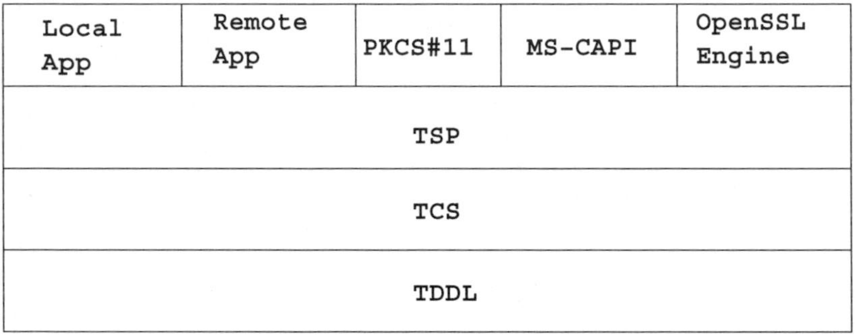

Local App	Remote App	PKCS#11	MS–CAPI	OpenSSL Engine
TSP				
TCS				
TDDL				

Figure 5.1: TSS Components

Beneath the TSS, a device driver is needed that was vendor specific for TPMs prior to the TPM 1.2 standard (TCG, 2007b). In order to have a more standardized interface, the TPM 1.2 specified a new interface called TCG PC Client Specific TPM Interface Specification (TIS), which is used now.

TPM commands sent through the TSS do not include any access control. It is up to the operating system to implement access control to the commands if desired.

5.3.2   Trusted Boot and Integrity Reporting with a TPM

As already mentioned in Section 5.2, the TCG has defined an algorithm for trusted booting. It has been mentioned that in contrast to secure systems, trusted systems can prove their trustworthiness. The owner is usually able to verify the trust herself since she knows the history of a platform, but a remote or roaming party needs other means to verify it. Therefore, the TCPA has specified a measurement algorithm that allows the local user as well as a remote party to verify the trust. As trust needs to be verified from the very first boot steps on, trusted platforms need a modified BIOS that includes a Root of Trust for Measurement (RTM). The RTM starts the measurement process and stores the results in a way that they cannot be undone. The reason why the Basic Input/ Output System (BIOS) is included is that a RTM only in the TPM would require a complete platform redesign, since this means the

TPM has to have control over the platform before the BIOS starts. In order to be able to access the TPM from the BIOS, the TPM has been attached to the Low Pin Count (LPC), which is also used to attach the system's BIOS flash memory. Like that, the TPM is available before any other device.

In general, the trusted boot process consists of several sequential measurement agents with the RTM being the first. Each agent measures the components it is responsible for, including the next agent, and stores the resulting report.

The entity keeping the reports in a secure way is called Root of Trust for Reporting (RTR). Besides storing the reports, the RTR prevents the release of platform state bound secrets if the measured values do not match the ones that are stored with the secret. In contrast to the RTM, the RTR is not implemented in the BIOS, but in the TPM and both – RTM and RTR/TPM – are the minimal roots of trust needed to implement measured boot. It ensures that a platform can reliably prove its integrity towards a remote or roaming party. The platform can even prove that it is able to reliably prove its integrity.

Obviously there has to be a way for the user to check whether someone has tampered with the TPM or not. If she cannot check this, she may accidentally trust a platform that is not trustworthy anymore. Such a tamper check can be realized by a broken seal or similarly, although it is very likely that no user will check the internal hardware of his computer before using it. Furthermore, a TPM can be audited and run a self-test to judge its trustworthiness.

The requirement for the TPM to be a cheap device leads to its coming with limited memory. Storing every result of the trusted boot process individually would require a huge amount of memory within the TPM, which is why only summaries are stored. A summary is a hash over a sequence of integrity measurements and is stored in a Platform Configuration Register (PCR). The individual results for each component of a trusted platform can be stored in software and checked against the summaries to find inconsistencies. Furthermore, there should be a measurement log containing the order of the measurements which is stored in the Trusted Platform Measurements Store (TPMS).

As already mentioned, a trusted platform can report its integrity metrics to another remote platform to prove its trustworthiness. An example for a possible integrity reporting protocol has been outlined in (Balacheff *et al.*, 2003) and works as follows:

1. The remote platform (*the challenger*) sends a nonce to the trusted platform that has to prove its trustworthiness (*the challenged platform*). That nonce is called *the integrity challenge.*

2. If the challenged platform accepts the nonce, it forwards the challenge to its TPM.

3. The TPM signs the nonce and the current PCR values that represent the challenged platform's state using a TPM identity (discussed below).

4. The Trusted Platform Agent (TPA – the entity on the challenged platform that handles the request from the challenger) retrieves the logs of the measured

software from the TPMS plus the certificates from the relevant repositories and bundles all together into the integrity response.

5. The challenger verifies the integrity of the response and inspects the certificates belonging to the challenged platform, the signed nonce, the signed PCRs, and the measurement logs.

There already are some special implementations of integrity checks for AMD Presidio and Intel LaGrande Technology CPUs that provide an option for going into secure mode to measure the trust of the rest of the system. Such a system cannot be emulated in software as it makes use of special LPC bus cycles (Challenger *et al.*, 2008).

5.3.3   Key Hierarchies in the TPM

Besides providing the RTR, the TPM includes a so called endorsement key that identifies a TPM uniquely worldwide. That key has to be injected during manufacturing. One way is to generate the key inside the TPM, which is probably the most trustworthy way, but it slows down the manufacturing process since generating RSA keys takes some time. Therefore it is also possible to generate the key outside the TPM and inject it afterwards (still at the manufacturer's). In order to be able to validate the trustworthiness of the endorsement key, there has to be an indicator that says whether the key has been generated inside or outside the TPM.

The endorsement key is used when taking ownership of a TPM in order to encrypt the owner's authorization secret and to send it securely to the TPM. The TPM that holds the private endorsement key is then the only entity that is able to decrypt the owner's secret. From this it follows that if a TPM allows remote ownership, the remote user needs to have the public endorsement key. During the taking ownership process, another key will be generated that serves as Storage Root Key (SRK) for all subsequently generated keys. Like this, a complete hierarchy of keys can be generated with one layer of keys wrapping all objects of the next layer. Only leafs of that hierarchy tree can be signing keys. If one of the wrapping keys is flagged as migratable, all keys and objects beneath that key are migratable too. Migration will be explained in the next section. Wrapping and unwrapping is done using asymmetric cryptography since the public key operation part of that process can be done outside the TPM and therefore achieve a far better performance.

The TPM knows several types of keys, such as *storage keys*, *signing keys* and *identity keys*. They all have different purposes and limitations. A *storage key* for instance is used as a wrapping key to encrypt key blobs – no matter whether the key blob includes a symmetric or an asymmetric key. Furthermore, a *storage key* can be used to encrypt data, which has to be SHA-1 or DER encoded for the time being. A *storage key* cannot be used to sign data. That is the purpose of a *signing key*, which can therefore not be used for wrapping. A key that is a combined storage and signing key is a *legacy key*, but those are not recommended (TCG, 2007b). *Legacy keys* have been introduced to support older applications that use one key for both. The reason why one should not use one key for both operations is that a *storage key* encrypts data using the public key, whereas signing is done by encrypting data using the private key. It follows that one could retrieve the clear text by doing the other operation (e.g. signing a stored object) using the same key.

Lastly there are *identity keys* that are special purpose keys that only sign data originating from inside the TPM. Identity keys are usually bound to a certain TPM and will never leave that special module. For the sake of completeness it has to be mentioned that there are also *binding*, *authchange*, and *migration keys*. *Binding keys* are used to bind data to the platform, *authchange keys* are used to change authorization information, and *migration keys* are used during the migration process explained below.

Aside from the purpose of a key, keys have other properties like a flag indicating whether they are *migratable* or not, or whether they require a usage secret or not.

5.3.4 Migration and Maintenance

Migration has been introduced to allow backups and the replacing of platforms without losing important information and secrets. Maintenance on the other hand has been designed to allow restoring broken TPMs and requires cooperation with the manufacturer of the TPM.

As already mentioned in Section 5.3.3, keys may be flagged *migratable*. Of course this does not apply to special purpose keys like *identity keys* that need to be bound to a certain TPM. A key flagged *migratable* can only be trusted by the entity that created it since nobody else knows its complete history and the intermediate (maybe even insecure) platforms the key has been migrated too. Migration is pretty open to misuse and should only be used carefully.

If a *storage key* is flagged *migratable*, all objects that have been wrapped using this *storage key* are *migratable* too. Migrating that key will cause all objects beneath it to be copied too.

Migration can be done directly or indirectly. Direct migration allows migrating a key (hierarchy) from one TPM to another TPM without intermediate entities. That means the destination TPM must be known and available during migration. The source TPM re-wraps the migratable key with the public key of the new parent key and sends the encrypted blob to the destination TPM, which is the only entity that is able to decrypt that blob. Indirect migration includes an intermediate entity that stores the encrypted blobs for an unspecified amount of time. In order to avoid revealing the migratable key to third parties or to the intermediate entity itself, the migratable object will be doubly encrypted. The inner encryption is done by the original owner, whereas the outer is done by the intermediate party.

Direct migration has been designed for cloning keys whereas indirect migration is more useful for backups, where you might not know the destination TPM in advance.

In order to reduce misuse, migration requires authorization, which is split into two steps: First of all, the entity that wants to migrate an object has to give the migration authorization secret for that object. Furthermore, the usage authorization secret for the public destination key is needed. It follows that the entity that has the migration secret for an object does not need to know the usage secret for that object. The latter might be known only to the user of a platform, whereas the migration secret is only known to the system administrator.

The migration functionality described above obviously requires a working source TPM at the moment the object is migrated. This is not the case if a TPM broke before a backup could be/ has been made. Furthermore, there are some objects like *identity keys* that cannot be migrated since they are bound to a certain TPM and that would be lost in case a TPM breaks. In order to cope with hardware failures, maintenance has been introduced as an optional feature. Maintenance requires the cooperation of the manufacturer of the TPM since it is a highly security critical process as it allows to clone a complete TPM. During maintenance, the Storage Root Key (SRK) of a TPM is converted into an encrypted object and injected into another TPM.

Since maintenance is such a critical process, the owner of a TPM may disable it. If disabled, it cannot be enabled again without erasing the owner in order to avoid misuse.

5.3.5   TPM Identities

In section 5.3.3, *identity keys* have been mentioned as special purpose keys with the property of not being migratable. This section explains *TPM identities* more detailedly.

TPM identities are so called *Identity or Attestation Identity Keys (AIKs)* that are signed by a special certificate authority called Privacy CA (PCA). *Identities* can prove that they belong to a genuine, given TPM. A user of a platform may have several TPM *identities* for several purposes, for instance one for online banking and another one for online shopping. The creation of a new *identity* requires the owner's secret whereas its use requires only the usage secret. It follows that one person, for instance the system's administrator, can create *identities* that will be used by other users of the platform. The administrator is not able to use the user's *identity* if the user does not reveal the usage secret.

Making sure that a TPM is genuine means that certain properties of the platform have to be guaranteed. These properties include the TCG capabilities and therefore provide enough evidence that the platform can report its integrity measurements trustworthily.

As already mentioned in 5.3.3, *identity keys* can only sign data that originates inside the TPM. This limitation has been introduced to prevent rogues from signing data and pretending that this data is trustworthy although it is not. Usually an *identity* is used to prove that data exists on a certain platform with a given state by signing data together with some PCR values with the *identity key*. Furthermore, one can sign other non-migratable keys (be it for storage or signing) that can then be trusted to originate from a certain TPM. This process is called key certification.

The public representation of an identity that can be verified by a third party is an X.509 certificate. If the TCG had not defined identity or AIK certificates, in order to achieve the same goals, a platform would have to send the Endorsement, PE, and CE certificate to identify itself, which raises privacy issues. As platforms may have different identity or AIK certificates for different purposes and as the PCA is the only party that is able to map them, the privacy problem has been solved with the introduction of identity certificates. Even the mapping at the PCA may be impossible if different PCAs are used for every *identity*.

(Challenger *et al.*, 2008) gives a pretty good overview of the protocol used to request a new identity certificate. A general overview will be shown in this chapter, whereas the technical details will be shown in Chapter 7.

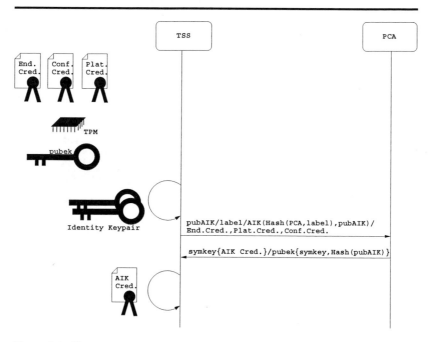

Figure 5.2: Identity Retrieval. pubek = public endorsement key, pubAIK = public identity key, K(x) = x signed with key K, Kx = x encrypted with key K

The protocol consists of six steps and involves three entities: The TPM itself, the Trusted Software Stack (TSS), and the signing PCA (see Figure 5.2):

TPM The TPM generates a new *identity key pair*, associates it with a certain PCA and a label given by the owner. This association is done by signing a hash over the label and the name of the PCA together with the new public key. The signature is done with the new identity public key.

TSS The TSS collects the endorsement, platform, and conformance credentials to be sent to the PCA together with so called *identity binding* created by the TPM in step 1.

PCA After the PCA has received all data collected in step 2, it verifies the information. At this point, the PCA cannot be sure that the request came from a
genuine TPM since it has not been signed with the endorsement key.

PCA In case the PCA is satisfied with the information it has received, a new identity
certificate will be issued. In order to make sure only a genuine TPM can cope
with the response, the new certificate will be encrypted using a symmetric
key which is then put together with a hash over the public identity key and
encrypted using the public endorsement key.

TPM The TPM decrypts the symmetric key and the hash. This step would fail if
there is no genuine TPM. If the encrypted hash matches the requested identity,
the TPM can be sure that identity has not been tampered with and releases
the symmetric key to the TSS, which then

TSS decrypts the identity certificate.

The identity certificate is now ready for use. It is obvious that this protocol
relies on the trustworthiness of the PCA. If the PCA misbehaves, the protocol will
break. This should not be an issue, since the PCA should be a trustworthy CA.

Step 4 makes use of the fact that an endorsement key proves that a platform is
genuine. As already mentioned, it is no must that the endorsement key has been
generated inside the TPM itself. It may have been generated outside and injected
later, but as there should be an indicator for that, it is up to the PCA to decide
whether it accepts the endorsement key or not.

The identity credential itself consists of

1. the statement that it is an identity credential,

2. a label that has been chosen by the owner to identify the credential,

3. a public identity key,

4. the specific type of the TPM and its security properties – both values copied
   from the endorsement credential –,

5. the specific type of the platform and its security properties – both copied from
   the platform credential –, and

6. the reference to the signing PCA.

As there is usually only one TPM per platform, an *identity* does not only identify
a TPM, but a platform. This fact has been used for the protocol described in the
next chapter.

The primary goal of AIKs is to report platform integrity metrics in a trustworthy
way. Usually platform metrics are signed using an identity key in order to make sure
they originate from a given platform.

5.4   Example Applications

The TPM can be used for a lot of applications like trusted boot, reliable random numbers etc. In 2007, (Latze & Ultes-Nitsche, 2007) specified an e-commerce authentication protocol that allows for a secure and comfortable e-commerce login. This protocol will be presented in Section 5.4.1.

Furthermore, IEEE 802.1AR (IEEE, 2009) presented in Section 3.3 also specifies how to use the TPM in order to implement secure network device identifiers, which will be discussed in Section 5.4.2.

5.4.1   Stronger Authentication in E-Commerce

As a part of this thesis, an authentication protocol using TPMs has been specified that shows how TPMs can lead to more usability in e-commerce applications while keeping a high level of security.

This protocol named *Stronger Authentication in E-Commerce* has been first specified in (Latze & Ultes-Nitsche, 2007) and (Latze, 2007). It has been developed in order to overcome security problems caused by phishing, pharming, and man-in-the-middle (MITM) attacks, which are the most common attacks on online applications. Phishing covers the social engineering attack where a user is tricked into revealing her credentials to an attacker. This happens mostly on faked online-banking or online-shopping websites that have been set up to collect user credentials. The user is usually tricked into navigating to such a website using emails that pretend to come from the real online bank or shop and request the user to confirm her credentials. The second attack is the pharming attack which includes DNS cache poisoning. A user who wants to connect to her online shop or bank will type the correct URL into her browser but will go to the wrong, faked website due to a poisoned cache. It is almost impossible for an inexperienced user to realize that there is an attack going on. Last, there are MITM attacks which require an attacker to install himself between a user and the server the user wants to communicate with in order to eavesdrop on the credentials exchanges between those two. Again, an inexperienced user would not recognize the MITM. It is often claimed that SSL/ TLS (Dierks & Rescorla, 2008) has been designed to solve these problems using certificates on the server side that allow a user to verify the server. In theory and from a technical point of view, this is a good solution, but browser warnings signaling a problem with the server are usually ignored by users as has been shown lately in (Sunshine *et al.*, 2009). Furthermore, even a malicious website might have a valid certificate. This would require the user to check the certificate in detail every time she connects to a server, which is far too time-consuming even for experienced users with a good technical knowledge. Therefore, SSL/ TLS is a good first step and should be used in any case, but it does not solve all problems, especially it cannot address problems caused by inexperienced users.

The attacks mentioned above only work so smoothly because standard user credentials only consist of username and password. If an attacker gets these credentials once, she is able to use them for anything in the future. It is getting even worse because users usually use the same username and password for several applications.

In order to make them unique, online banks add so called Transaction Numbers (TANs) or RSA SecurIDs (RSA Security, 2009). But these, too, cannot avoid the attacks mentioned above. Even a MITM is still possible at least for the lifetime of the token of the TAN list or generated by the SecurID. From the server's point of view, an attacker using these credentials cannot be distinguished from a legitimate user since there is no parameter that is unique to the user.

The author of this thesis proposed in (Latze & Ultes-Nitsche, 2007) to use the TPM to make the user unique. In order to do so, the TPM is used to

1. ensure the e-commerce application's integrity on the client side. That may include the operating system as well. This is done to prevent the user from using malicious software.

2. bind the user to certain credentials.

3. ensure a specific hardware is used for authentication in order to detect an attacker who would likely connect from another hardware.

Although those features could also be implemented using standard smart cards, TPMs are preferred over smart cards since they are built into almost every new computer. Therefore, in contrast to smart cards, TPMs are ubiquitous devices/ modules.

The protocol proposed in (Latze & Ultes-Nitsche, 2007) does also provide a fallback for users who do not have a computer with a TPM or for users who want to access the online shop or bank from another computer. The fallback provides the possibility to authenticate using the user's mobile phone since those are ubiquitous devices too.

In order to provide a really secure setup that is suitable for online banking as well, (Latze & Ultes-Nitsche, 2007) proposes to register the user in advance using signed snail mail. The bank sends a CD-ROM to the user with the following content:

1. the e-commerce provider's public key with a piece of software sealing the key to the TPM of the clients machine,

2. a piece of software for client key generation, printing the client's public key's fingerprint and sealing the client's private key in the TPM. The printed fingerprint will be sent to the merchant by registered mail for key verification. Since the e-commerce provider needs to scan the public AIK in that scenario, one might also think about a secure upload provided on the CD-ROM.

3. the e-commerce software using user credentials *and* a mutually authenticated challenge-response protocol where verification of the merchant's authentication information and computation of the client's authentication information is done by the TPM.

It has to be mentioned that such a complex registration procedure is only useful for applications that require high security like online banking. Furthermore, such

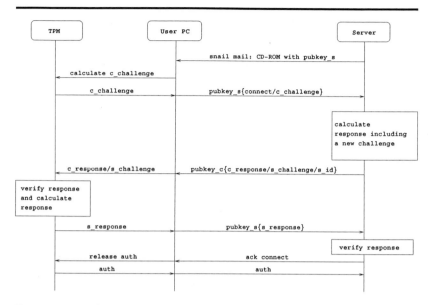

Figure 5.3: The Authentication Process from the User's Registered Home Machine.

applications are usually the ones that a user uses for a long time. Online shops that a user uses only once do not need such a complex registration.

Figure 5.3 shows the authentication protocol run when using a TPM. It starts with the TPM calculating c_challenge, which is used to authenticate the e-commerce server. Afterwards, the user tries to connect to the e-commerce server and sends c_challenge encrypted with the server's public key. The server authenticates itself by calculating the appropriate response c_response. That includes decrypting c_challenge using the server's private key as well as encrypting the response using the client's public key. Furthermore, the server sends a new challenge s_challenge to the client to authenticate it. That message also includes the server's ID. Otherwise the protocol would be vulnerable to Man-in-the-Middle (MITM) attacks. Using the TPM, the application on the user's machine verifies the server's response c_response and calculates a new response s_response for s_challenge. The application on the user's computer asks the TPM to release the user credentials, which was sealed to a successful server authentication. The application sends the authentication information to the e-commerce provider.

The fallback using mobile phones requires the user to register her phone number at the e-commerce provider. According to (Latze & Ultes-Nitsche, 2007), there are two versions of this fallback:

1. Using mobile phones that are able to run third party software, and

2. using mobile phones that are not able to run additional software.

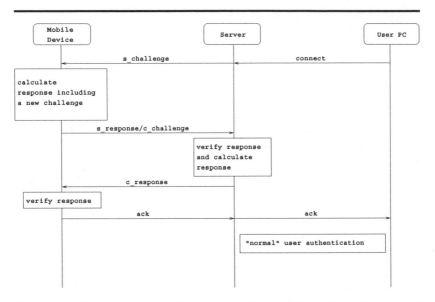

Figure 5.4: The Authentication Process when Using a Mobile Phone Running 3rd Party Software.

Figure 5.4 shows the protocol when running third party software. The mobile phone plays the role of the TPM, which may even be enforced by using the SIM to secure the application. Furthermore, with the emergence of Mobile Trusted Modules (MTMs) (TCG, 2008), the devices may provide better security anyway. Since the algorithm shown in Figure 5.4 does only secure the connection between the mobile phone and the server, the user will get transaction confirmation messages on her mobile phone for every transaction she does. Even if an attacker eavesdrops or modifies the traffic between the user's computer and the server, she cannot do any harm to the user.

Figure 5.5 shows an algorithm using simple One Time Passwords (OTPs) since such a protocol can be implemented on every mobile phone. Again, this fallback needs a transaction confirmation SMS for every transaction the user does.

In (Latze *et al.*, 2009c), the author provides a security proof using the AVISPA framework (AVISPA, 2009). The result of that proof was that nobody can impersonate the client and the nonces exchanged during authentication are never released to an attacker. Therefore, the protocol can be considered secure.

In 2009, a proof of concept implementation has been finished and evaluated (Ruppen, 2009). The implementation proved to be easy and transparent for the user.

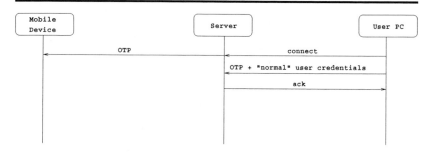

Figure 5.5: The Authentication Process when Using Old Mobile Phones.

It has been shown that the protocol can be smoothly integrated into applications providing the standard user authentication using username and password.

Furthermore, it has been shown that the time needed to authenticate a user using a TPM is about 4.7 seconds, which is little. Obviously it takes more time when using a mobile phone, but even then, average values of 19.5 seconds for the OTP solution and 27.1 seconds for the more complex mobile phone based solution have been reached.

Concluding, *Stronger Authentication in E-Commerce* is a promising approach to providing more security in online user authentication using TPMs. However, the offline key exchange in the beginning may be uncomfortable and would probably be used in high risk setups only.

5.4.2 Using a TPM to Implement Wireless Network Device Identifiers

Chapter 3 discussed the IEEE 802.1AR standard that does also specify how to implement a DevID with the help of a TPM. This section gives an overview of the TPM features needed to be compliant with IEEE 802.1AR.

Recalling, the required features of a DevID module are:

1. There is an initial IDevID injected by the manufacturer.

2. It should be possible to define LDevIDs.

3. There must be cryptographic storage.

4. It must be possible to create, import, and control the usage of asymmetric keys.

5. It must be possible to enable and disable the DevID.

6. The DevID secret must be a 2048 bit RSA key.

7. Hashes must be calculated using SHA-256.

A TPM comes with a so called endorsement key and credential, but these cannot be used for authentication. This means that a device manufacturer has to create a further identity credential serving as IDevID during the manufacturing process. Accordingly, in the future, a factory fresh TPM has to be initialized, enabled, and owned, if it is to be used for DevID enabled applications. As the TPM is able to bind cryptographic keys to a device, the first IDevID meets the IEEE 802.1AR standard.

LDevIDs on a TPM can be implemented as Attestation Identity Keys (AIKs), which are non-migratable keys bound to a certain device. Furthermore, a TPM does provide the required cryptographic storage as well as the creation, import, and controlled usage of an unlimited number of asymmetric cryptographic keys. The enabling and disabling of the DevIDs inside a TPM can be implemented by enabling or disabling the module itself.

According to IEEE 802.1AR, a DevID secret must be RSA 2048 bit, which is possible using a TPM, although the optional feature of ECC secrets cannot be provided by TPMs.

The IEEE requires SHA-256 to be used for all credentials which is not implemented in the current TPMs. However, it is possible to use the PKCSv1 DER encoding interface and inject externally generated SHA-256 hashes to be signed.

The main problem with using the TPM to implement a DevID is that IEEE 802.1AR requires a DevID to be usable with standard authentication protocols. However, the use of TPMs in such protocols may need slight modifications of the protocols as proposed for TLS in Chapter 6.

5.5   Interim Conclusion

The Trusted Computing Group (TCG) specified the Trusted Platform Module (TPM) in order to establish a root of trust in consumer hardware. The features of the TPM can be used for several applications starting from simple encryption/ decryption up to authentication in computer networks. Two authentication applications have already been shown in this chapter. A third one that can be used in public wireless networks will be shown in the next chapter.

6
Using the TPM in EAP-TLS

Besides using the TPM as trusted device to run a challenge-response based authentication protocol as described in Section 5.4.1, it is possible to use the TPM as an identification device itself, which is also the idea behind IEEE 802.1AR. The motivation behind this approach is that users want to use IEEE 802.11 networks in the same comfortable and secure way they use GSM/ UMTS networks today. Chapter 2 outlines the technical details of GSM and UMTS networks. Figure 2.1 and 2.3 show the complex technical architecture of GSM and UMTS networks. User authentication in both networks is done by authenticating the SIM card which is bound to a user by contract. That makes the networks very comfortable from a user's point of view. Usually, all a user does is to buy a SIM card and a mobile phone, insert the SIM card, and switch on the mobile phone. Afterwards, the user is able to call people and to receive calls or to open data connections in case of UMTS. The reason for this good usability is that there is only one SIM authentication protocol that is used in every GSM network. Furthermore, the user is bound to his SIM(s) by signing a contract at an operator. The situation is different for wireless LANs since most of the wireless LANs are controlled by private people who do not need user authentication and accounting. With the emergence of public wireless LANs, users need to be authenticated in a secure and comfortable manner in order to be charged or to be identified in case of misuse or a criminal incident. That requires a secure and comfortable authentication scheme comparable to GSM/ UMTS networks. The solution proposed in this thesis uses the Trusted Platform Module (TPM) described in Section 5.3 to provide at the least the same level of security as in GSM/ UMTS networks by using a trusted piece of hardware in addition to a mutual authentication method. Furthermore, the goal was to provide the same good usability in wireless LANs as in GSM/ UMTS networks.

In order to meet those goals, the authentication scheme proposed in this thesis uses the Attestation Identity Keys (AIKs) introduced in Section 5.3.5 in EAP-TLS presented in Section 4.2.3.

The remainder of this Chapter will start with a short motivation, followed by a detailed discussion of the TLS handshake including the proposal about how to integrate the TPM. Afterwards, a few possibilities to retrieve the AIKs are discussed. The Chapter concludes with accounting and roaming issues.

6.1   Motivation

Chapter 4 discusses the authentication methods used in today's public wireless LANs. EAP-TLS is one of the best authentication methods regarding security if used with mutual authentication. However, the need for client certificates prevents it from being deployed widely. Requesting an X.509 certificate is a complicated process as shown in Section 4.2.3 – probably too complicated for normal users. That is one of the reasons why a lot of other authentication methods have been specified that provide some kind of workaround. EAP-SIM is one of them and replaces the client certificate with the SIM credentials.

This chapter aims at developing a solution for using EAP-TLS in a more comfortable way without the need to abandon client certificates. The approach presented in this chapter makes use of the TPM to generate and store certificates in a more user-friendly way.

The TPM and its features have been presented in Chapter 5. There are several possibilities for using a TPM in TLS based protocols like EAP-TLS. First of all, a non-migratable key could be created that has to be signed by a CA in order to get a client certificate for TLS. However, although such a scheme already introduces more security than a software-only solution, it is still not very user-friendly. Generating a standard RSA key and requesting a certificate for that key at a standard CA is the same as in software. This is different for AIK certificates as outlined in Section 5.3.5. Such certificates come with a different, more user-friendly, requesting process. Furthermore, as shown in Section 5.4.2, AIK certificates have been identified as valid network device IDs. It has therefore been decided to use AIK certificates in TLS to implement a user-friendly and secure public wireless authentication method.

6.2   The TLS TPM Extension

Section 4.2.3 has already given a short introduction to TLS, but in order to have a complete understanding of the problems when using TPMs in TLS, the important information will be repeated in this section.

TLS has been developed to allow for a secure transport between two entities. Most of the time, it will be sufficient to authenticate the server, but TLS allows for client authentication too. Since the authentication scheme proposed in this thesis requires mutual authentication, this section will only cover mutual authentication properties of TLS.

The newest version of TLS is TLS 1.2 as specified in (Dierks & Rescorla, 2008), although most of the implementations running today will only support TLS 1.1. One of the most common implementations of TLS, called OpenSSL (OpenSSL, 2009), does not even support TLS 1.2 until today. The general handshake messages remain the same in TLS 1.1 and TLS 1.2 and are shown in Figure 6.1 (copied from Section 4.2.3 for a better readability).

During the handshake, RSA signing is required which is defined differently in TLS 1.1 and TLS 1.2. For TLS 1.1 as specified in (Dierks & Rescorla, 2006), RSA signing is defined as:

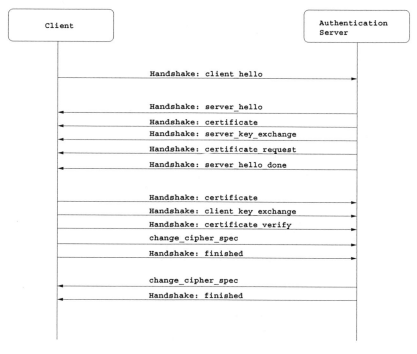

Figure 6.1: TLS Handshake

"In RSA signing, a 36-byte structure of two hashes (one SHA and one MD5) is signed (encrypted with the private key)."

In order to do that with TPM signing keys, the TSS_TSPATTRIB_KEYINFO_SIG-SCHEME parameter of that key needs to be set to TSS_SS_RSASSAPKCS1V15_DER, which is not possible for AIKs. TLS 1.2 has redefined the signature method:

"In RSA signing, the opaque vector contains the signature generated using the RSASSA-PKCS1-v1_5 signature scheme defined in [PKCS1]. As discussed in [PKCS1], the DigestInfo MUST be DER-encoded [X680] [X690]. For hash algorithms without parameters (which includes SHA-1), the DigestInfo.AlgorithmIdentifier.parameters field MUST be NULL, but implementations MUST accept both without parameters and with NULL parameters. Note that earlier versions of TLS used a different RSA signature scheme that did not include a DigestInfo encoding."

This is standard RSA signing, which in theory is also possible with AIKs. The only problem when using AIKs to sign data is that this data must originate within the TPM. It follows that the hash which is signed has to originate inside the TPM.

To store the hash inside a TPM's PCR is quite an overhead just to be able to sign it using an AIK. Furthermore, signing a PCR is done by signing the PCR value as well as the PCR number. Using a PCR in a TLS handshake would therefore require more changes to the handshake. Accordingly, the goal was to use another key that is somehow related to the AIK for TLS. The four possibilities that have been studied and evaluated for this thesis are presented and discussed in the next sections.

6.2.1   Certified Keys

In order to overcome the problem of the limited features of the Attestation Identity Keys (AIKs), the Trusted Computing Group (TCG) have presented their own solution called *certified keys* specified in (TCG, 2006a). *Certified keys* are keys that are signed by a TPM key, for instance using the AIK. In case a key is certified with the AIK, it is non-migratable and therefore proven to be held "in a TPM shielded location and will never be revealed" (TCG, 2006b). However, it is no must to certify keys only with the AIK, it is also possible to use signing and legacy keys to certify migratable keys also. *Certified keys* may have any property that is needed for the current application, in particular they may use the TSS_SS_RSASSAPKCS1V15_DER signing scheme which is required for TLS 1.1. Furthermore, those keys can be used to sign external data, which was a requirement too.

Coming back to TLS authentication in wireless LANs, one of the requirements was to be able to prove that a certain device has been used. Obviously this requires the use of a non-migratable key, which requires AIK signed *certified keys*. It follows, that AIK signed *certified keys* fulfill all the requirements for TLS 1.1 and TLS 1.2 authentication and are therefore a good choice for the authentication scheme discussed in this thesis. However, the representation of these keys is a problem. The term *certified key* suggests that these keys are stored in X.509 certificates, which is unfortunately not true. An X.509 certificate as specified in (Cooper *et al.*, 2008) has the following format:

```
Certificate  ::=  SEQUENCE  {
  tbsCertificate       TBSCertificate,
  signatureAlgorithm   AlgorithmIdentifier,
  signatureValue       BIT STRING  }

TBSCertificate  ::=  SEQUENCE  {
  version           [0]  EXPLICIT Version DEFAULT v1,
  serialNumber           CertificateSerialNumber,
  signature              AlgorithmIdentifier,
  issuer                 Name,
  validity               Validity,
  subject                Name,
  subjectPublicKeyInfo SubjectPublicKeyInfo,
  issuerUniqueID    [1]  IMPLICIT UniqueIdentifier OPTIONAL,
          -- If present, version MUST be v2 or v3
```

```
subjectUniqueID [2]   IMPLICIT UniqueIdentifier OPTIONAL,
        -- If present, version MUST be v2 or v3
extensions       [3]  EXPLICIT Extensions OPTIONAL
        -- If present, version MUST be v3
}
```

whereas on the other hand, the TPM_CERTIFY_INFO structure holding the properties of the *certified key* looks like this:

```
typedef struct tdTPM_CERTIFY_INFO{
    TPM_STRUCT_VER              version;
    TPM_KEY_USAGE              keyUsage;
    TPM_KEY_FLAGS             keyFlags;
    TPM_AUTH_DATA_USAGE        authDataUsage;
    TPM_KEY_PARMS              algorithmParms;
    TPM_DIGEST                pubkeyDigest;
    TPM_NONCE                 data;
    BOOL                      parentPCRStatus;
    UINT32                    PCRInfoSize;
    [size_is(pcrInfoSize)] BYTE*  PCRInfo;
} TPM_CERTIFY_INFO;
```

Additionally, there is the signature itself.

Although both structures carry somewhat similar information, they are far from being identical. Within the next sections, several valid representations of the *certified key* are discussed and evaluated.

6.2.2 Subject Key Attestation Evidence X.509 Extension

In 2005, the Trusted Computing Group (TCG) have released their own solution to this problem called Subject Key Attestation Evidence (SKAE) (The Trusted Computing Group, 2005). Their goal was to integrate the concept of *certified keys* into the standard X.509 PKI in order to be able to use standard protocols without or with only slight modifications. SKAE is an X.509 certificate extension carrying the TPM_CERTIFY_INFO structure as well as the AIK's signature which can be added by certificate authorities (CAs). Furthermore, the SKAE extension includes the information of where to get the AIK in order to be able to verify TPM_CERTIFY_INFO. The following listing shows the format of the SKAE extension:

```
SubjectKeyAttestationEvidence ::= SEQUENCE {
    tcgSpecVersion         TCGSpecVersion,
    keyAttestationEvidence KeyAttestationEvidence
}

KeyAttestationEvidence ::= CHOICE {
    attestEvidence           [0] AttestationEvidence,
    envelopedAttestEvidence  [1] EnvelopedAttestationEvidence
```

```
}

AttestationEvidence ::= SEQUENCE {
  tpmCertifyInfo                TPMCertifyInfo,
  tpmIdentityCredAccessInfo  TPMIdentityCredentialAccessInfo
}

TCGSpecVersion ::= SEQUENCE {
  major INTEGER,
  minor INTEGER
}

TPMCertifyInfo ::= SEQUENCE {
  CertifyInfo  BIT STRING,
  signature    BIT STRING
}
```

Since the structure may change with newer TCG specifications, it is important to mention the version `TCGSpecVersion` used to create the specific extension. Afterwards, it has to be decided whether one wants to send the extension in clear, which results in setting `AttestationEvidence`, or whether the content has to be encrypted, which results in `EnvelopedAttestationEvidence`. The details of the encryption are explained in (The Trusted Computing Group, 2005) and will not be repeated here since they do not help to understand the concept. The content is the same as for the cleartext version. `AttestationEvidence` carries the `TPM_CERTIFY_INFO` structure as well as access information to the AIK that was used to sign this *certified key*. That may be for instance a LDAP location. The AIK certificates are handled like CA certificates which means there needs to be some kind of centralized storage for them (probably at the PCA).

The process of obtaining a certificate with the SKAE extension is the following:

1. The client generates a new AIK and

2. sends it to the Privacy CA (PCA) in order to get an AIK certificate.

3. Afterwards, the client generates a new non-migratable TPM key,

4. signs it using the AIK,

5. creates a new certificate request including the SKAE extension, and

6. sends the new request to a CA,

7. that signs it and sends the certificate back.

The result is a valid X.509 certificate on the client side that can be used for instance for TLS. However, there are several issues with that approach:

First of all it requires two certificate requests – one for the AIK and one for the *certified key*. Even if a user decides to create several *certified keys* beneath one AIK, the second certificate request carrying the SKAE extension is somehow an overkill. The AIK is already a trusted and valid X.509 certificate, and the name "certified key" implies that the AIK certificate is used as local CA. The only reason why an AIK cannot sign the SKAE extended *certified key* certificate directly is that the AIK certificate has the "CA:false" constraint as specified in (TCG, 2002).

Furthermore, a server that wants to authenticate a client sending a certificate with the SKAE extension has to retrieve the client's AIK certificate from a location specified within SKAE by itself. Again this is a very complicated process compared to standard certificate based authentication, where the client sends the complete chain.

Concluding, it has been decided not to use SKAE for the wireless authentication scheme developed in this thesis for the following reasons:

1. The requirement for a new CA signed certificate carrying the SKAE extension introduced unacceptable complexity. One of the advantages of *certified keys*, that is the local creation of new trustable certificates, will be lost using the SKAE architecture. A client would always need a connection to a CA, although all the local components are already trustworthy.

2. The need for the server to retrieve the AIK certificate itself introduced even more complexity. This is especially a problem because for privacy reasons, it is desirable to delete the client's AIK as soon as possible. If the same client connects again using the same *certified key*, the server has to retrieve the same AIK again since caching is not recommended.

So, due to the complexity introduced with SKAE, other approaches have been evaluated.

6.2.3   X.509 Proxy Certificates

In 2004, the IETF published the concept of X.509 proxy certificates as proposed standard (Tuecke *et al.*, 2004). The idea behind X.509 proxy certificates is to give some rights of the original certificate to a proxy certificate which will then be used in applications like authentication. A proxy certificate may even have a shorter lifetime than the original certificate. Proxy certificates will not be signed by a CA, but by the original client certificate (or another proxy certificate).

At first sight, this looks exactly like what is needed for representing *certified keys* as valid X.509 certificates without too much additional complexity. But (Tuecke *et al.*, 2004) defines several constraints for the original certificate that must be met, like for instance in Section 3.1 of (Tuecke *et al.*, 2004): "The Proxy Issuer MUST NOT have an empty subject field." The proxy issuer here is the client's AIK certificate whose subject field is NULL according to (TCG, 2002). This collides with the requirements for these certificates in (Tuecke *et al.*, 2004) and does therefore prevent the usage of X.509 proxy certificates in the authentication scheme presented in this thesis.

6.2.4   TPM Certificates

Sections 6.2.2 and 6.2.3 have shown that it is rather complicated to make TPM_CER-
TIFY_INFO fit into existing X.509 structures. This is only possible by introducing
an unacceptable degree of complexity as shown in Section 6.2.2. Therefore, in 2009,
(Latze *et al.*, 2009b) and (Latze & Ultes-Nitsche, 2008) defined a new certificate
format called *TPM Certificate* that represents a *certified key*. The new certificate
looks quite similar to X.509, but carries all the information needed for *certified keys*:

```
Certificate ::= SEQUENCE {
    parentSerialNumber      CertificateSerialNumber,
    pubKey                  OCTET STRING,
    tpmCertificate          TPMCertificate,
    tpmSigLen               INTEGER,
    signatureValue          BIT STRING
}


TPMCertificate ::= SEQUENCE {
    versionMajor            OCTET,
    versionMinor            OCTET,
    versionRevMajor         OCTET,
    versionRevMinor         OCTET,
    keyUsage                OCTET STRING,
    keyFlags                OCTET STRING,
    authDataUsage           OCTET,
    algorithmID             OCTET STRING,
    encScheme               OCTET STRING,
    sigScheme               OCTET STRING,
    parmSize                INTEGER,
    parms           [0]     OCTET STRING OPTIONAL,
        --If not present, parmSize MUST be 0--
    pubkeyDigest            OCTET STRING,
    nonce                   OCTET STRING,
    parentPCRStatus         BOOLEAN,
    PCRInfoSize     [1]     INTEGER OPTIONAL,
        --If not present, parentPCRStatus MUST be FALSE--
    PCRInfo         [2]     OCTET STRING OPTIONAL,
        --If not present, parentPCRStatus MUST be FALSE--
}
```

The *TPM Certificate* carries the AIK's serial number in order to be able to
reproduce the chain again. Furthermore, as in every X.509 certificate, it includes
the *certified key's* public key as well as the signature of the parent certificate. In
addition to an X.509 certificate it does also carry the TPM_CERTIFY_INFO structure
as an integral part of the certificate. This is the main difference to SKAE where
TPM_CERTIFY_INFO is carried in the extensions. The complete chain *X.509 PCA root
certificate → X.509 AIK certificate → TPM certificate* has to be stored and loaded

from a file name `<whatever>.tpm` in order to send and use the complete chain. Like in the PEM format mentioned in (Korver, 2007), the individual certificates are Base64 encoded and stored between `-----BEGIN CERTIFICATE-----` and `-----END CERTIFICATE-----`. During the TLS handshake, the certificates will be sent by the client in order for the server to be able to verify the complete chain.

By defining a new certificate, all the problems arising from existing formats have been solved, but such a new format requires a lot of change in current TLS libraries. Even if it is possible to implement an authentication scheme based on new certificates in a small network such as a company network, it will never be usable in big public wireless networks as it requires too many changes on the clients. Therefore, work on *TPM certificates* has been stopped in order to find a more standard conform possibility.

6.2.5 TLS TPM Extension

In 2006, the IETF released a new standard called "TLS Handshake Message for Supplemental Data" (Santesson, 2006). A supplemental data handshake message allows to send data that has been announced using TLS hello message extensions. The extensions concept has been defined in (Dierks & Rescorla, 2008) and allows, together with the supplemental data handshake message, to extend the TLS handshake in a standard compliant and backwards compatible way. Entities – be it client or server – who do not implement the extensions just ignore them.

The general idea of the TLS TPM extension specified in (Latze *et al.*, 2009d) is to announce the usage of self-signed *certified keys* using the hello message extensions, and to send the AIK certificate using the supplemental data handshake message in order to verify the self-signed *certified key*.

In order to use the *certified key* as-is in the TLS handshake, a self-signed certificate has to be generated that carries the SKAE extension with `AttestationEvidence.TPMIdentityCredentialAccessInfo` set to NULL. This self-signed *certified key* certificate is used with the standard TLS handshake. In order to be able to verify the *certified key* against its AIK certificate, a TLS extension has been specified to announce the use of AIK certificates. The general TLS extension message looks like this:

```
struct {
  ExtensionType extension_type;
  opaque extension_data<0..2^16-1>;
}
```

Since AIK and *certified key* certificates may be used on both sides, the TLS TPM extension type has been defined as follows:

```
enum {
  client_aik(TBD), server_aik(TBD), (65535)
} ExtensionType
```

As (Latze *et al.*, 2009d) is still a work in progress, there is no IANA number assignment so far, which leads to "TBD" (To Be Determined) instead of numbers.

With (TCG, 2006a), the TCG introduced an additional certify information structure called `TPM_CERTIFY_INFO2`. Since older TPMs do only support `TPM_CERTIFY_INFO`, in order for the other protocol entity to be able to know which structure is hidden within the *certifed key's* SKAE extension, the `extension_data` part of the extension message carries:

```
enum {
  tpm_certify_info(0), tpm_certify_info2(1), (255)
} CertifyInfoType
```

One might argue that the TCG specification version number is already included in the SKAE extension, but relying on the version number only is not sufficient, since for instance (TCG, 2006a) defines both structures. That means a TPM compliant with (TCG, 2006a) is able to create both structures. Therefore, in order to be sure to expect the right format, the structure used is announced in `CertifyInfoType`. The extension messages are exchanged during the first two messages of a TLS handshake as shown in Figure 6.2.

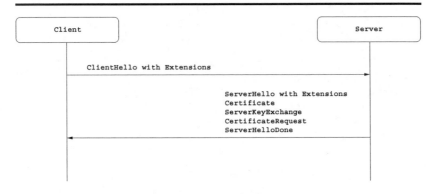

Figure 6.2: TLS Extensions

After having agreed on using the AIK on either one or both sides, the AIK has to be sent with the supplemental data handshake message:

```
enum {
  aik_data(TBD), (65535)
}

struct {
  SupplementalDataType supplemental_data_type;
  select(SupplementalDataType) {
    case aik_data: AikData;
  }
```

```
} SupplementalData

opaque ASN.1Cert<2^24-1>;

struct {
  ASN.1Cert certificate_list<0..2^24-1>;
} AikData;
```

This message is the third message of the TLS handshake. Figure 6.3 shows the complete TLS handshake including the extension and supplemental data handshake messages.

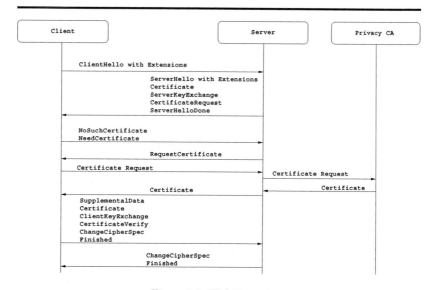

Figure 6.3: TLS Extensions

Assuming a client wants to use a *certified key* certificate whereas the server uses standard X.509 certificates, the protocol run would look like this:

1. The client announces the desire to use a self-signed *certified key* certificate by sending a hello extension with `client_aik` set.

2. In case the server accepts that authentication, he replies with the extension with `client_aik` set.

3. Later, the client includes his AIK certificate into the supplemental data handshake message and sends it to the server.

4. The server is now able to verify the self-signed *certified key* certificate.

Since this approach is standard conform, backwards compatible and does not introduce an unacceptable amount of complexity, it has been chosen as the perfect solution for the authentication scheme for wireless networks proposed in this thesis.

6.3   Identity Retrieval

In order for the client to be able to authenticate in a public wireless network, it needs to have an AIK first. The process of obtaining a new AIK has already been described in Section 5.3.5 and will not be repeated here. This section concentrates on the user's point of view.

For a user, there are mainly two possibilities to retrieve a new identity:

1. Using a special client software that has been installed and does everything from generating and releasing the new identity key on the local platform up to communicating with a PCA to get the key signed. In this case, the algorithm described in Section 5.3.5 runs between the user's PC and the PCA.

2. The provider of a public wireless LAN might provide a webportal that allows to download software to generate and release the key locally. The user has to upload the output of the software, which is the certificate request, to the webportal which communicates with then a PCA. In this case, the algorithm described in Section 5.3.5 runs between the server running the webportal and the PCA.

No matter which solution has been chosen, the process always starts with obtaining a new AIK. Afterwards, both solutions generate a new TLS key locally (this is the new *certified key* with the signing scheme set to TSS_SS_RSASSAPKCS1V15_DER), certify it using the AIK, and self-sign it using any TLS library.

Both solutions have been implemented and evaluated as will be shown in Section 7.2.

6.4   Roaming and Accounting

Since the authentication scheme presented in this thesis has been designed for public wireless networks, it is necessary to think about the basics of accounting too. The technical implementation of accounting is done using AAA protocols like RADIUS or DIAMETER and has already been explained in Section 4.3.1. This section deals with the general requirements for accounting in public wireless networks. Roaming is implicated by accounting and will be discussed in Section 6.4.2.

6.4.1   Accounting

Accounting in public wireless networks is needed since such networks are usually controlled by an operator who will hardly allow users to access the network for free. As already mentioned, the authentication scheme presented above allows to

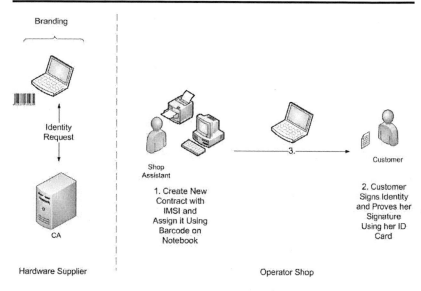

Figure 6.4: How to Bind a User to her Device when Buying a New Device

authenticate the device, not the user. Therefore, in order to charge a user, the device needs to be bound to a user.

Figure 6.4 shows how the binding may be done at the time a user buys a device like a notebook. It is assumed that the user does not have any contract with the operator yet. The process works similarly to the process of selling new SIM cards. A notebook already comes pre-initialized with an identity that is stored in the operator's database for that device. If a user buys the device, the device will be simply assigned to this user who in addition signs a contract with the operator.

Since there are also users who want to buy their devices in other shops or who want to use devices they already own, there is another registration procedure as shown in Figure 6.5. Again it is assumed that the user does not have any contract with the operator so far. The user takes her device and enters the operator's shop, where a new contract has to be created. In order to be able to request a new valid identity for the user's device, the shop assistant assigns the user a PIN that is needed to connect to a dedicated hotspot in the shop. The user has to enter the PIN at the hotspot's captive portal and is then allowed to request a new AIK using that hotspot. Obviously, there is only one connection possible via this access point, namely the connection to the operator's PCA. The PCA is coupled to the operator's contract database and is therefore able to assign the identity to the new user by searching the PIN the user had to enter. Lastly, the contract is signed by the user.

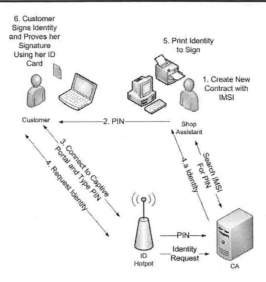

Figure 6.5: How to Bind a User to her Device Using an Existing Device

Both Figures 6.4 and 6.5 mention an IMSI that has to be assigned to the new user. As shown in Chapter 2, IMSIs are identifiers for GSM or UMTS networks, but not for wireless networks. The reason why the IMSI is also used for wireless networks in this proposal is that operator management systems are usually IMSI based due to legacy reasons.

Lastly, the user who wants to request a new identity for an existing device may already have a contract with the operator (maybe for her mobile phone). This can be covered using the standard captive portal that is provided by every public hotspot to allow access for users without contract. In order to get access to the Internet to request a new identity, the user authenticates herself using her existing ID with the operator, e.g. her mobile phone number. Section 6.3 discusses two possibilities for implementing the client software for AIK retrieval that have been programmed.

6.4.2 Roaming

Roaming covers the mobility of users from the network managed by operator A to a network managed by operator B. There are two possibilities for the user:

1. If A and B have signed a roaming agreement, the user may use her identity received from operator A in the domain of B too. That means that operator B knows and accepts the PCA of operator A. B is therefore able to verify the identity of the user.

2. If A and B do not have a roaming agreement or if the user wants to save money, she can retrieve another identity for operator B.

In GSM/ UMTS networks, the second case implies a new SIM card and probably a new mobile phone too. In TPM authenticated wireless LANs, this is not necessary anymore. One TPM may store several identities or AIKs for several purposes. It is then up to the user to decide whether she wants to sign different contracts with different operators or not. Furthermore, in GSM/ UMTS networks, a user who had different SIM cards for different operators did also have different phone numbers, which is quite uncomfortable. In wireless LANs, communication between two or more users is usually done using applications like VOIP or chat that have their own identities, which are unrelated to the network identity. Therefore, roaming in TPM authenticated wireless LANs will be much more comfortable than it was in GSM/ UMTS.

6.5 TPM Supported Zero Configuration for Wireless Computer Networks

All the authentication protocols used so far in IEEE 802.11 networks require the distribution or retrieval of user credentials before the first connect of an user. Obviously when talking about commercial public wireless LANs, such a pre-authentication process is absolutely necessary. However, there might be cases when such a pre-authentication process does only introduce more complexity. One could imagine a company network where all new devices are registered and whitelisted using their MAC address. Since MAC filtering is not very secure, it might be desired to reconfigure the devices automatically on first connect to use EAP-TLS with the TPM extension. Since the TPM is a trusted entity that can be identified uniquely worldwide, it was possible to develop a zero-configuration scheme for TPM support authentication that allows retrieving an AIK during the first connect. The zero-configuration scheme has been implemented by modifying the TLS handshake a bit (Latze *et al.*, 2008).

Figure 6.6 shows the time-line of the TLS handshake used in TPM assisted authentication as it is used in EAP-TLS with TPM extensions. The handshake starts with the `ClientHello` message containing the version of the TLS protocol on the client's side, a random number that will be used to generate session keys, a session ID in order to indicate a session to resume (has to be omitted for new sessions), the supported cipher suites and the supported compression algorithms. The server responds with a `ServerHello` message containing the protocol's version number on the server's side, a random number, the session ID that may be used by the client to resume that session at a later time, the supported cipher suites and the supported compression algorithms. Afterwards, the server sends its own X.509 certificate in the `Certificate` message. As EAP-TLS with the TPM extension uses mutual authentication, the next step is the `CertificateRequest` message in order to request the client's certificate. Besides including the type of the requested certificate – the server may chose between RSA and DSS signatures – the server may

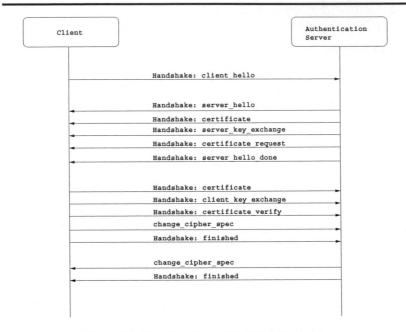

Figure 6.6: Time-line Unmodified TLS Handshake

also specify the acceptable CAs. In order to realize the zero-configuration scheme, this feature will be used to transmit the acceptable PCAs. After having received this message, the client has to check whether it has an identity issued by one of these PCAs or not. In case it does not have such an identity, it may request a new identity on-the-fly and go on with the handshake afterwards.

Figure 6.7 shows the details of the modified handshake described above. As in an unmodified TLS handshake, it starts with a ClientHello and a ServerHello. Afterwards, the server sends the Certificate message followed by a CertificateRequest containing the acceptable PCAs. The structure of CertificateRequest does not change:

```
struct {
  ClientCertificateType
    certificate_types<1..2^8-1>;
  DistinguishedName
    certificate_authorities<3..2^16-1>;
}CertificateRequest
```

The PCAs have to be specified in the certificate_authorities section of this message. The ServerHelloDone indicates the end of the handshake. Now the client

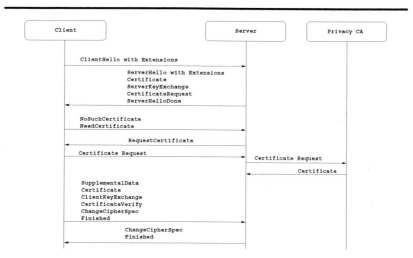

Figure 6.7: Timeline Modified TLS Handshake

has to check whether it has an appropriate identity or not. In case it has one, the handshake goes on as shown in Figure 6.6, but in case it does not own such an identity, it sends an alert message `NoSuchCertificate`. The general structure of an alert message in TLS is as follows:

```
struct {
  AlertLevel level;
  AlertDescription description;
}Alert
```

where `AlertLevel` is defined as

```
enum{warning(1),fatal(2),(255)}AlertLevel;
```

For the `NoSuchCertificate` alert, an `AlertLevel` of `warning` would be appropriate because according to the TLS standard, an alert message with the level `fatal` causes an immediate shutdown of the session (Dierks & Rescorla, 2008). That would abort the zero-configuration as well.

For the alert description, TLS already defines 24 fixed possibilities:

```
enum {
 close_notify(0),
 unexpected_message(10),
 bad_record_mac(20),
 decryption_failed(21),
```

```
record_overflow(22),
decompression_failure(30),
handshake_failure(40),
no_certificate(41),
bad_certificate(42),
unsupported_certificate(43),
certificate_revoked(44),
certificate_expired(45),
certificate_unknown(46),
illegal_parameter(46),
unknown_ca(48),
access_denied(49),
decode_error(50),
decrypt_error(51),
export_restriction(60),
protocol_version(70),
insufficient_security(71),
internal_error(80),
user_cancelled(90),
no_renegotiation(100),
(255)
} AlertDescription;
```

The `no_certificate` option was only supported in SSLv3 but indicates a missing certificate as desired for zero-configuration. Therefore, one could use this alert in TLS to indicate that the client does not have a certificate of one of the acceptable PCAs. Afterwards, the client has to send the `NeedCertificate` message in order to determine which PCA he wants to use:

```
struct {
  opaque privacy_ca<1..2^16-1>;
}NeedCertificate
```

The server will now ask the client for its certificate request message and request the certificate at the desired PCA on behalf of the peer. He starts the certificate request process with a `request_certificate` message:

```
struct {
  ConnectionAllowed allowed;
  opaque privacy_ca<1..2^16-1>;
}request_certificate
```

where

```
enum {
  true(1), false(2)
}ConnectionAllowed
```

The client must check the `privacy_ca` value. If it does not match the PCA specified in `need_certificate`, the peer must close the authentication immediately. If the `privacy_ca` value matches and allowed is set to `true`, the client is allowed to request a new certificate. It sends its `certificate_request` message described in Section 5.3.5 to the server, which will then request the peer's certificate at the PCA. The PCA sends the client's certificate back to the server, which will forward the certificate to the client in the `client_certificate` message. Afterwards, the client has to generate the self-signed *certified key* certificate in order to be able to use that one for authentication. In the original TLS handshake shown in Figure 6.6, the final `Finished` message includes digests over all the handshake messages in order to prove integrity. Of course, all these new handshake messages have to be included into the digest too.

The implementation and evaluation details of the zero-configuration scheme are discussed in Sections 7.4 and 8.2.

6.6 Correctness Proofs

In order to show the correctness of the TLS TPM extension as well as of the zero-configuration protocol, mathematical proofs are given that are based on the logic presented in (Durgin *et al.*, 2001) and used in (He *et al.*, 2005) to prove the correctness of EAP-TLS and IEEE 802.11i. (He *et al.*, 2005) is also referred to in (Simon *et al.*, 2008) as the EAP-TLS proof.

6.6.1 Protocol Composition Logic

In 2007, the authors of PCL wrote a summary of their logic and published it in (Datta *et al.*, 2007). A slightly different syntax is used in (He *et al.*, 2005) to prove the correctness of IEEE 802.11i including TLS. That is why this thesis uses the syntax of (He *et al.*, 2005) to be consistent with the TLS proof.

This section will explain all the details of the Protocol Composition Logic (PCL) needed to be able to understand the proofs.

Every role of a protocol can be modeled in the form $\theta[P]_X\tau$ with θ being a precondition and P some actions of the role during a protocol run. After the run, τ holds. The notation $[]_X$ describes the actions of an instance X of the protocol participant $\hat{X}$. PCL knows the following actions:

- send m - send the message m

- receive x - receive a message into variable x (NB: (He *et al.*, 2005) uses the following syntax for receiving a message into a variable:
  receive x;
  match x/M;
  where M is the expected message)

- new n - generate a new term n

- match u/v - match a term to a pattern

- $x:=\mathtt{sign}\ u, K$ - sign term u with key K and store the result in x

- $\mathtt{verify}\ s, u, K$ - verify the signature s of term u using key K

- $x:=\mathtt{enc}\ u, K$ - encrypt the term u with key K and store the result in x

- $x:=\mathtt{dec}\ u, K$ - decrypt the term u with key K and store the result in x

Every action that includes an X (without hat) is an action which is valid for a certain protocol run, whereas actions including an $\hat{X}$ (with hat) are valid for the principle itself. A good example for this distinction is the signing of a nonce n vs. the signing of a public key (a certificate). A signature is denoted by $SIG_K(t)$, which means a key K signed a term t, with a term being the data to be signed (e.g. a public key in case of a certificate). A nonce n belongs to a certain protocol session, which is why its signature looks like this: $SIG_K(X, n)$. However a certificate (that is a signature of a public key) belongs to a principle and is used in different sessions, which leads to $SIG_{\hat{CA}}(\hat{X}, K_{\hat{X}})$. In addition to the principle itself, $\hat{X}$ denotes the public key of the participant $\hat{X}$. $\bar{X}$ describes the private key.

Every action in PCL has an appropriate action predicate that holds in a run if the matching action has been executed, e.g. if session X executes the action $\mathtt{send}$ t, the predicate $Send(X, t)$ holds. The term t that is sent includes the IDs (that is most likely the IP addresses) of the protocol participants: $t = (\hat{X}, \hat{Y}, Message)$. In the proof itself, the predicate will therefore be written as $Send(X, \hat{X}, \hat{Y}, Message)$. Another example for a predicate is $Verify(X, t)$, which holds if X executes the action $\mathtt{verify}\ t, u, K$ with $t = SIG_K(u)$. In addition to $Send(X, t)$ and $Verify(X, t)$, PCL knows $Receive(X, t)$, $New(X, t)$, and $Decrypt(X, t)$. Furthermore, there is the predicate $Has(X, t)$, which is used to state secrecy properties. $Has(X, t)$ means that X has either generated t or received it in an encrypted way where X has the decryption key. $Has(X, t)$ is characterized by the following six axioms:

- **ORIG** $New(X, t) \supset Has(X, t)$

- **REC** $Receive(X, t) \supset Has(X, t)$

- **TUP** $Has(X, t) \wedge Has(X, s) \supset Has(X, (t, s))$

- **ENC** $Has(X, t) \wedge Has(X, K) \supset Has(X, ENC_K(t))$

- **PROJ** $Has(X, (t, s)) \supset Has(X, t) \wedge Has(X, s)$

- **DEC** $Has(X, ENC_K(t)) \wedge Has(X, K) \supset Has(X, t)$

Colloquially spoken, **ORIG** says that X has a term t if it has created it. **REC** states that X has t if it has received it. **TUP** and **PROJ** state that if X has two terms t and s, it knows the tuple of them and vice versa. **ENC** and **DEC** deal with encryption and decryption and require that X has the appropriate key K in addition to the term t.

Furthermore, PCL knows a predicate $Honest(\hat{X})$ which states that all actions executed by $\hat{X}$ are prescribed by the protocol. Lastly, there is the predicate $Nonce$

$Source(X, n, ENC_K(n))$, which says that a principle $\hat{Y}$ that generates a value n in thread Y sends it only encrypted.

In addition to the possession axioms presented above, PCL knows the following axioms that are needed in the proofs presented in the next sections. $\top$ denotes the boolean value *true*.

- **AA4** $\top[a; ...; b]_X a < b$ - After a thread X executes the actions $a; ...; b$ in that order, the appropriate predicates are temporally ordered too.

- **AN2** $\top[\text{new } x]_X Has(Y, x) \supset (Y = X)$ - If X creates a new term x and does not send it, no other thread knows it.

- **ARP** $Receive(X, x)[\text{match } x/t]_X Receive(X, t)$ - If X has received x that matches t, X received t is valid.

- **SEC** $Honest(\hat{X}) \wedge Decrypt(Y, ENC_{\hat{X}}(x)) \supset (\hat{Y} = \hat{X})$ - The private key is needed to decrypt a message x, and the private key will never leave the principle $\hat{X}$ it belongs to if $\hat{X}$ is honest.

- **VER** $Honest(\hat{X}) \wedge Verify(Y, SIG_{\hat{X}}(x)) \wedge \hat{X} \neq \hat{Y} \supset \exists X.Send(X, SIG_{\hat{X}}(x))$ - Signatures are unforgable and can only be verified on the principle $\hat{X}$ that created it or on $\hat{Y}$ if $\hat{Y}$ has received it from $\hat{X}$.

Besides these basic axioms of PCL, a new axiom **SIG** has been defined:

- **SIG** $Honest(\hat{Y}) \wedge New(X, m) \wedge Receive(X, \hat{Z}, \hat{X}, SIG_{\hat{Y}}(m)) \supset \hat{Z} = \hat{Y}$

SIG states that if something is generated in a protocol run, signed by a known entity $\hat{Y}$ and received in the session X that generated it, the signed message must originate at $\hat{Y}$. This is true since $\hat{Y}$ is honest and does therefore keep its private key secret.

Last, the TPM is assumed to be trusted since this is the basis of the protocols presented in this thesis.

Those are the basic axioms needed to prove the correctness of the TLS TPM extension in Section 6.6.2 and of the zero configuration protocol given in Section 6.6.3.

6.6.2 TLS TPM Extension

(He *et al.*, 2005) shows a proof of standard TLS, which can be used as a base for the proof of the TLS TPM extension. In (He *et al.*, 2005), the TLS client and server are modelled as follows:

$$
\begin{aligned}
TLS\, Client =& (X, \hat{Y}, VerSU_X)[\\
& \text{new } N_X; \\
& \text{send } \hat{X}, \hat{Y}, N_X, VerSU_X;
\end{aligned}
$$

$\qquad$ receive $\hat{Y}, \hat{X}, N_Y, VerSU_Y, cert;$

$\qquad$ match $cert/SIG_{\hat{C}A}(\hat{Y}, K_Y);$

$\qquad$ new $secret;$

$\qquad$ send $\hat{X}, \hat{Y}, SIG_{\hat{C}A}(\hat{X}, V_X),$

$\qquad$ $SIG_{V_X}(handShake1), ENC_{K_Y}(secret),$

$\qquad$ $HASH_{secret}(handShake1, ``client'');$

$\qquad$ receive $\hat{Y}, \hat{X}, hash;$

$\qquad$ match $hash/HASH_{secret}(handShake2, ``server'');]_X$

$TLS\ Server = (Y, VerSU_Y)[$

$\qquad$ receive $\hat{X}, \hat{Y}, N_X, VerSU_X;$

$\qquad$ new $N_Y;$

$\qquad$ send $\hat{Y}, \hat{X}, N_Y, VerSU_Y, SIG_{\hat{C}A}(\hat{Y}, K_Y);$

$\qquad$ receive $\hat{X}, \hat{Y}, cert, sig, encsec, hash;$

$\qquad$ match $cert/SIG_{\hat{C}A}(\hat{X}, V_X);$

$\qquad$ match $sig/SIG_{V_X}(handShake1);$

$\qquad$ match $encsec/ENC_{K_Y}(secret);$

$\qquad$ match $hash/HASH_{secret}(handShake1, ``client'');$

$\qquad$ send $\hat{Y}, \hat{X}, HASH_{secret}(handShake2, ``server'');]_Y$

This model exactly matches the TLS handshake for mutual authentication as specified in (Dierks & Rescorla, 2008) and shown in Figure 4.13. Before starting the handshake, a client knows the server $\hat{Y}$ he wants to connect to. Furthermore, it knows its TLS version number and acceptable ciphersuites $VerSU_X$, and obviously it knows its session X too. The server does "only" know his TLS version number and acceptable ciphersuites $VerSU_Y$ as well as its session Y.

The handshake is started by the client sending its version number and the possible ciphersuites hidden in $VerSU_X$ as well as a nonce N_X. Afterwards it receives the server's certificate $SIG_{\hat{C}A}(\hat{Y}, K_Y)$ and verifies it: `match` $cert/SIG_{\hat{C}A}(\hat{Y}, K_Y)$. Next, it sends its own certificate $SIG_{\hat{C}A}(\hat{X}, V_X)$, a session key $secret$ as well as the $finished$ message that hashes all the handshake messages sent so far:

$HASH_{secret}(handShake1, ``client'')$.

Last, the client verifies the server's $finished$ message:

`match` $hash/HASH_{secret}(handShake2, ``server'')$.

The strings $``client''$ and $``server''$ are the $finished\ labels$.

(He $et\ al.$, 2005) proves that session authentication and the secrecy of $secret$ are fulfilled for this model.

In order to prove the same for TLS TPM extension, several steps have to be added to the client and server roles that represent the handshake extension as well as the supplemental data handshake message:

$$TLS\ Client = (X, \hat{Y}, VerSU_X)[$$

new N_X;

send $\hat{X}, \hat{Y}, N_X, VerSU_X,$ "aik", "clientaik", "certit";

receive $\hat{Y}, \hat{X}, N_Y, VerSU_Y, extt, extd1, extd2, cert$;

match $extt/$"aik";

match $extd1/$"clientaik";

match $extd2/$"certit";

match $cert/SIG_{\hat{CA}}(\hat{Y}, K_Y)$;

new $secret$;

send $\hat{X}, \hat{Y}, SIG_{P\hat{C}A}(\hat{X}, A_{\hat{X}}), SIG_{\hat{X}}(\hat{X}, V_X),$

$SIG_{V_X}(handShake1), ENC_{K_Y}(secret),$

$HASH_{secret}(handShake1,$ "client");

receive $\hat{Y}, \hat{X}, hash$;

match $hash/HASH_{secret}(handShake2,$ "server"); $]_X$

The client extends its `client_hello` with the extension *aik* that includes the indicator that the client wants to use an AIK certificate *clientaik* as well as the special `TPM_CERTIFY_INFO` structure that will be used. After the server has acknowledged the extension with can be verified by match $extt/$"aik"; match $extd1/$"clientaik"; match $extd2/$"certit";, the client sends its AIK certificate as supplemental data handhake message: $SIG_{P\hat{C}A}(\hat{X}, A_{\hat{X}})$. $A_{\hat{X}}$ denotes the client's AIK key. Last of all, the client sends the self-signed *certified key* $SIG_{\hat{X}}(\hat{X}, V_X)$ as part of the certificate message. The rest of the handshake is the same as in standard TLS.

The server needs some more steps too:

$$TLS\ Server = (Y, VerSU_Y)[$$

receive $\hat{X}, \hat{Y}, N_X, VerSU_X,$ "aik", "clientaik", "certit";

new N_Y;

send $\hat{Y}, \hat{X}, N_Y, VerSU_Y,$ "aik",

"clientaik", "certit", $SIG_{\hat{CA}}(\hat{Y}, K_Y)$;

receive $\hat{X}, \hat{Y}, certaik, cert, sig, encsec, hash$;

match $certaik/SIG_{P\hat{C}A}(\hat{X}, A_{\hat{X}})$;

match $cert/SIG_{\hat{X}}(\hat{X}, V_X)$;

match $V_X/certic$;

match $certic/TPMSIG_{A_X}(\hat{X}, V_X)$;

match $sig/SIG_{V_X}(handShake1)$;

match $encsec/ENC_{K_Y}(secret)$;

$$\text{match } hash/HASH_{secret}(handShake1, \text{``}client\text{''});$$
$$\text{send } \hat{Y}, \hat{X}, HASH_{secret}(handShake2, \text{``}server\text{''});]_Y$$

The server receives the client's wish to use the TLS TPM extension and acknowledges it. After having received the client's AIK certificate $SIG_{P\hat{C}A}(\hat{X}, A_{\hat{X}})$ as well as the self-signed *certified key* certificate $SIG_{\hat{X}}(\hat{X}, V_X)$, a new verification procedure takes place. Instead of a simple match $cert/SIG_{\hat{C}A}(\hat{X}, V_X)$ as in standard TLS, three verifications are needed:

1. match $certaik/SIG_{P\hat{C}A}(\hat{X}, A_X)$, in order to verify the client's AIK certificate, which is signed by a publicly know Privacy CA.

2. match $cert/SIG_{\hat{X}}(\hat{X}, V_X)$, in order to verify the self-signed certificate that is used by the client to sign the *finished* message, and

3. match $certic/TPMSIG_{A_X}(\hat{X}, V_X)$, in order to verify the *certified key*. The syntax $TPMSIG$ has been choosen to denote a TPM *certified key*.

It remains to show that the few changes listed above do not violate the session authentication and the key secrecy proven in (He *et al.*, 2005). This is done by proving that the following invariants still hold for every new action:

$$\Gamma_{tls,1} := \neg\exists m.Send(X, m) \wedge (Contains(m, HASH_{secret}(handShake1, \text{''}server\text{''})) \vee$$
$$Contains(m, HASH_{secret}(handShake2, \text{''}client\text{''})) \vee$$
$$Contains(m, SIG_{V_X}(handShake1)))$$

$$\Gamma_{tls,2} := Honest(\hat{Y}) \wedge Send(Y, m) \wedge ContainsOut(m, secret, ENC_{K_Y}(secret)) \supset$$
$$(\neg Decrypts(Y, m') \wedge Contains(m', secret)) \vee$$
$$(Receives(Y, m'') < FirstSend(Y, secret) \wedge$$
$$ContainsOut(m'', secret, ENC_{K_Y}(secret)))$$

$\Gamma_{tls,1}$ states that no other protocol should create and send out the *finished* message. Neither the client modifications nor the server modifications do anything like this.

$\Gamma_{tls,2}$ says that the *secret* can be sent out in clear only if it has been received in clear before. Again, neither the client nor the server modifications change that invariant. The *secret* is not transmitted over any hidden channel.

Summarizing, the changes that are needed to implement the TLS TPM extensions do obviously only affect the certificate verification on the server side, which is why the proof of TLS as shown in (He *et al.*, 2005) is still applicable. There are no changes to the TLS handshake that change the secrecy of *secret* or the session authentication.

6.6.3 Zero Configuration

The zero configuration protocol as specified in Section 6.5 can be separated into two protocols:

1. The TLS protocol that has already been proven in (He *et al.*, 2005), and

2. the AIK certificate retrieval as specified by the TCG.

The proof of the latter is still open and will be done in this section. It is again based on the logic presented in (Durgin *et al.*, 2001) and the protocol will be denoted with $ZERO$ in the proof.

Given the notation in Section 6.6.1, the client of a protocol $ZERO$ specified in Section 5.3.5 can be modelled with the client being $\hat{X}$ and the server (that is the PCA) $\hat{Y}$ as follows:

$$
\begin{aligned}
Client = & (X, \hat{Y})[\\
& new A_{\hat{X}}; \\
& send\ \hat{X}, \hat{Y}, A_{\hat{X}}, "label", \\
& SIG_{\bar{A}_{\hat{X}}}(HASH(\hat{Y}, "label")), A_{\hat{X}}), SIG_{T P\hat{M}E}(\hat{X}, E_{\hat{X}}), \\
& SIG_{\bar{P}E}(\hat{X}, P_{\hat{X}}), SIG_{\bar{C}E}(\hat{X}, C_{\hat{X}}); \\
& receive\ \hat{Y}, \hat{X}, encaik, encsym; \\
& match\ encsym/ENC_{E_{\hat{X}}}(symkey, HASH(A_{\hat{X}})); \\
& symkey, hash := dec\ ENC_{E_{\hat{X}}}(symkey, HASH(A_{\hat{X}})), \bar{E}_{\hat{X}}; \\
& match\ hash/HASH(A_{\hat{X}}); \\
& match\ encaik/ENC_{symkey}(SIG_{\hat{Y}}(\hat{X}, A_{\hat{X}}); \\
& cert := dec\ ENC_{symkey}(SIG_{\hat{Y}}(\hat{X}, A_{\hat{X}})), symkey;]_X
\end{aligned}
$$

The precondition $(X, \hat{Y})$ describes the current instance X as well as the fact that the client does already know the server (that is the PCA) it wants to connect to: $\hat{Y}$. The first action of the client is to send some data to the PCA with $\hat{X}$ being the source address and $\hat{Y}$ the destination address. $A_{\hat{X}}$ denotes the public AIK key that has to be signed. In order to get it signed, the client has to send $A_{\hat{X}}$ as well as a label denoted by *"label"*, the endorsement credential $SIG_{T P\hat{M}E}(\hat{X}, E_{\hat{X}})$ signed by the Trusted Platform Module Entity (TPME), the platform credential $SIG_{\bar{P}E}(\hat{X}, P_{\hat{X}})$ signed by the Platform Entity (PE), and the conformance credential $SIG_{\bar{C}E}(\hat{X}, C_{\hat{X}})$ signed by the Conformance Entity (CE) to the Privacy CA (PCA). Furthermore, the message includes a hash over the PCA's public key $\hat{Y}$ and the AIK key $A_{\hat{X}}$, which is signed with the AIK key $A_{\hat{X}}$. It has to be mentioned that $P_{\hat{X}}$ and $C_{\hat{X}}$ do not contain keys but rather vouchers for the platform as described in Section 5.2. Both vouchers together state that the TPM has been implemented and attached to the motherboard according to the standards. These vouchers are the basis for the trust in the TPM.

Afterwards, the client will receive a message from the PCA ($\hat{Y}$ being the source and $\hat{X}$ the destination) containing two parameters $encsym$ and $encaik$. $encsym$ carries $ENC_{E_{\hat{X}}}(symkey, HASH(A_{\hat{X}}))$, which includes the symmetric key $symkey$ created by the PCA $\hat{Y}$, and a hash over the client's public AIK key $A_{\hat{X}}$, both encrypted using the client's public endorsement key $E_{\hat{X}}$. Since the client has the private endorsement key $\bar{E}_{\hat{X}}$, it is able to decrypt the message:

$symkey, hash :=$dec $ENC_{E_{\hat{X}}}(symkey, HASH(A_{\hat{X}})), \bar{E}_{\hat{X}}$. Afterwards, it compares the hash $hash$ with the expected result $HASH(A_{\hat{X}})$ and uses $symkey$ to decrypt the new AIK certificate:

$cert :=$dec $ENC_{symkey}(SIG_{P\hat{C}A}(\hat{X}, A_{\hat{X}})), symkey;$.

As discussed in Section 5.3.5, some of the actions described above are executed on the TPM and can therefore be assumed to be trusted. These actions are:

$$new A_{\hat{X}};$$
$$x := \text{sign } (HASH(\hat{Y}, "label"), A_{\hat{X}}), \bar{A}_{\hat{X}};$$
$$symkey, hash := \text{dec } ENC_{E_{\hat{X}}}(symkey, HASH(A_{\hat{X}})), \bar{E}_{\hat{X}};$$
$$\text{match } hash/HASH(A_{\hat{X}});$$
$$cert := \text{dec } ENC_{symkey}(SIG_{\hat{Y}}(\hat{X}, A_{\hat{X}})), symkey;]_X$$

The server (PCA) role can be modelled as follows:

$$Server =(Y)[$$
$$\text{receive } \hat{X}, \hat{Y}, A_{\hat{X}}, "label", aiksig, certek, certp, certconf;$$
$$\text{match } aiksig/SIG_{\bar{A}_{\hat{X}}}(HASH(K_{\hat{Y}}, "label"), A_{\hat{X}});$$
$$\text{match } certek/SIG_{TP\hat{M}E}(\hat{X}, E_{\hat{X}});$$
$$\text{verify } SIG_{TP\hat{M}E}(\hat{X}, E_{\hat{X}}), TP\hat{M}E;$$
$$\text{match } certp/SIG_{\hat{P}E}(\hat{X}, P_{\hat{X}});$$
$$\text{verify } SIG_{\hat{P}E}(\hat{X}, P_{\hat{X}}), \hat{P}E;$$
$$\text{match } certconf/SIG_{\hat{C}E}(\hat{X}, C_{\hat{X}});$$
$$\text{verify } SIG_{\hat{C}E}(\hat{X}, C_{\hat{X}}), \hat{C}E;$$
$$aikc := \text{sign } (\hat{X}, A_{\hat{X}}), \hat{Y};$$
$$\text{new } symkey;$$
$$\text{send } \hat{Y}, \hat{X}, ENC_{symkey}(aikc), ENC_{E_{\hat{X}}}(symkey, HASH(A_{\hat{X}}));]_Y$$

The server does only know its actual instance but not the client. It receives all the data and starts by verifying the endorsement, platform, and conformance credential:

```
verify SIG_{TPME}(X̂, E_X̂), TPM̂E;
verify SIG_{PE}(X̂, P_X̂), P̂E;
verify SIG_{CE}(X̂, C_X̂), ĈE;
```

Next, it signs the public AIK key: $aikc :=$ `sign` $(\hat{X}, A_{\hat{X}}), \hat{Y}$; which assigns $aikc$ the value $SIG_{\hat{Y}}(\hat{X}, A_{\hat{X}})$. As already mentioned, the PCA has to make sure that the new certificate can only be read by the TPM equipped client that sent the request, which is why a new symmetric key $symkey$ is generated that is used to encrypt the certificate. In order to transmit the key securely over the network, the key itself is concatenated with a hash over the $A_{\hat{X}}$ and encrypted using the client's public endorsement key $E_{\hat{X}}$.

There are two definitions that result out of this protocol model:

Definition 1

The certificate retrieval completes successfully if $\phi_{zero,aik}$ holds, where :

$$\phi_{zero,aik} ::= Honest(\hat{X}) \wedge Honest(\hat{Y}) \supset$$
$$\exists Y.ActionsInOrder($$
$$Send(X, \hat{X}, \hat{Y}, Message1),$$
$$Receive(Y, \hat{X}, \hat{Y}, Message1),$$
$$Send(Y, \hat{Y}, \hat{X}, Message2),$$
$$Receive(X, \hat{Y}, \hat{X}, Message2))$$

This definition states that the order of the messages sent in a protocol run cannot change if $\hat{X}$ and $\hat{Y}$ are *honest*.

Definition 2

The request is said to provide key secrecy if $\phi_{zero,sec}$ holds, where :

$$\phi_{zero,sec} ::= Honest(\hat{X}) \wedge Honest(\hat{Y}) \supset$$
$$(Has(Z, symkey) \supset Z = X \vee Z = Y) \wedge$$
$$Has(X, symkey) \wedge Has(Y, symkey)$$

Definition 2 states that the symmetric key $symkey$ generated by the PCA is only known to X and Y.

Furthermore, there is one precondition θ_{zero} and one invariant Γ_{zero} for the certificate request:

$$\theta_{zero} := NonceSource(Y, symkey, ENC_{E_{\hat{X}}}(symkey)) \wedge$$
$$(Decrypts(Z, ENC_{\hat{X}}(m)) \supset \hat{Z} = \hat{X}) \tag{6.1}$$

which states that the symmetric key $symkey$ is only sent out under encryption with the client's public endorsement key $E_{\hat{X}}$. This is denoted by the predicate

NonceSource (He, 2006). Furthermore, since the client $\hat{X}$ is equipped with a TPM that stores the private keys, messages encrypted with the client's public key can only be decrypted by the client itself. The invariant

$$\Gamma_{zero} := Honest(\hat{X}) \wedge Receive(X, Message) \supset \neg Send(X, Message) \qquad (6.2)$$

states that client and PCA are running on different machines since the source and the destination instance of a *Message* are never the same.

Based on these assumption, the following theorem can be defined:

Theorem

> $On\ execution\ of\ the\ protocol\ ZERO\ -\ defined\ by$
> $Client\ and\ Server\ -,\ key\ secrecy\ and$
> $certificate\ retrieval\ are\ guaranteed\ if\ the\ invariant$
> $and\ the\ precondition\ hold:$
> $\Gamma_{zero} \vdash \theta_{zero}[ZERO]_X \phi_{zero,aik} \wedge \phi_{zero,sec}.$

In order to provide the final proof, one can reason as follows:

AA4 Since the client is honest, it knows that its own actions are in order. Since the server's actions are based on input given by the client, it cannot send a message before receiving the request of the client, which results in
$Send(X, \hat{X}, \hat{Y}, A_{\hat{X}}, ''label'', SIG_{\bar{A}_{\hat{X}}}(HASH(\hat{Y}, ''label'')), A_{\hat{X}}),$
$SIG_{T\hat{P}ME}(\hat{X}, E_{\hat{X}}), SIG_{\hat{PE}}(\hat{X}, P_{\hat{X}}), SIG_{\hat{CE}}(\hat{X}, C_x) <$
$Receive(X, \hat{Y}, \hat{X}, ENC_{symkey}(SIG_{\hat{Y}}(\hat{X}, A_{\hat{X}})), ENC_{E_{\hat{X}}}(symkey, HASH(A_{\hat{X}})))$

(6.2),Honest($\hat{X}$) After the client has received the encrypted AIK certificate, it can be sure there was some entity $\hat{Z}$ who computed and sent out the message:
$\theta_{zero}[receive\ \hat{Y}, \hat{X}, encaik, encsym;$
match $encsym/ENC_{E_{\hat{X}}}(symkey, HASH(A_{\hat{X}}));$
match $encaik/ENC_{symkey}(SIG_{\hat{Z}}(\hat{X}, A_{\hat{X}}));]_X$
$Receive(X, \hat{Y}, \hat{X}, ENC_{E_{\hat{X}}}(symkey, HASH(A_{\hat{X}})), ENC_{symkey}(SIG_{\hat{Z}}(\hat{X}, A_{\hat{X}}))) \supset$
$Send(Z, \hat{Z}, \hat{X}, ENC_{E_{\hat{X}}}(symkey, HASH(A_{\hat{X}})), ENC_{symkey}(SIG_{\hat{Z}}(\hat{X}, A_{\hat{X}}))) \wedge$
$(Send(Z, \hat{Z}, \hat{X}, ENC_{E_{\hat{X}}}(symkey, HASH(A_{\hat{X}})), ENC_{symkey}(SIG_{\hat{Z}}(\hat{X}, A_{\hat{X}}))) <$
$Receive(X, \hat{Z}, \hat{X}, ENC_{E_{\hat{X}}}(symkey, HASH(A_{\hat{X}})), ENC_{symkey}(SIG_{\hat{Z}}(\hat{X}, A_{\hat{X}}))))$

ENC,REC In order to be able to encrypt and send the message, $\hat{Z}$ must know *symkey*:
$Has(Z, ENC_{E_{\hat{X}}}(symkey, HASH(A_{\hat{X}}))) \equiv Has(\hat{Z}, symkey) \wedge$
$Has(\hat{Z}, HASH(A_{\hat{X}})) \wedge Has(\hat{Z}, E_{\hat{X}});$
$Has(Z, HASH(A_{\hat{X}})) \equiv Has(\hat{Z}, A_{\hat{X}});$
$Has(Z, ENC_{symkey}(SIG_{\hat{Z}}(\hat{X}, A_{\hat{X}}))) \equiv Has(\hat{Z}, symkey) \wedge Has(\hat{Z}, A_{\hat{X}});$

ORIG,DEC If $\hat{Z}$ knows $symkey$, it must be either X or Y:
$Has(\hat{Z}, symkey) \equiv New(Z, symkey) \vee$
$Decrypts(Z, ENC_{E_{\hat{X}}}(symkey, HASH(A_{\hat{X}}))) \supset Z = X \vee \exists Z.New(Z, symkey)$

(6.2) But since X does not send these messages, Z cannot be X:
$\theta_{zero}[\text{receive } \hat{Y}, \hat{X}, encaik, encsym;]_X$
$Honest(\hat{X}) \wedge$
$Receive(X, \hat{Y}, \hat{X}, ENC_{E_{\hat{X}}}(symkey, HASH(A_{\hat{X}})), ENC_{symkey}(SIG_{\hat{Z}}(\hat{X}, A_{\hat{X}}))) \supset$
$Z \neq X$

ORIG,AN2,(6.1),SIG Z must be Y (since $symkey$ is generated by Y and sent only in an encrypted message, decryptable by X only): $Honest(\hat{X}) \wedge Honest(\hat{Y}) \supset$
$\exists Z.Has(Z, ENC_{E_{\hat{X}}}(symkey, HASH(A_{\hat{X}}))) \wedge$
$Has(Z, ENC_{symkey}(SIG_{\hat{Y}}(\hat{X}, A_{\hat{X}}))) \wedge$
$Send(Z, \hat{Z}, \hat{X}, ENC_{E_{\hat{X}}}(symkey, HASH(A_{\hat{X}})), ENC_{symkey}(SIG_{\hat{Y}}(\hat{X}, A_{\hat{X}}))) \wedge$
$Z = Y$

Honest($\hat{X}$) Furthermore, the message has been encrypted and sent before the client X received it: $Honest(\hat{X}) \wedge Honest(\hat{Y}) \supset$
$Send(Y, \hat{Y}, \hat{X}, ENC_{E_{\hat{X}}}(symkey, HASH(A_{\hat{X}})), ENC_{symkey}(SIG_{\hat{Z}}(\hat{X}, A_{\hat{X}}))) <$
$Receive(X, \hat{Y}, \hat{X}, ENC_{E_{\hat{X}}}(symkey, HASH(A_{\hat{X}})), ENC_{symkey}(SIG_{\hat{Z}}(\hat{X}, A_{\hat{X}})))$

REC Since the message sent by Y requires Y to process data received from X, Y must have this sequence: $Honest(\hat{X}) \wedge Honest(\hat{Y}) \supset$
$Receive(Y, \hat{X}, \hat{Y}, A_{\hat{X}}, SIG_{TPME}(\hat{X}, E_{\hat{X}}), SIG_{\hat{PE}}(\hat{X}, P_{\hat{X}}), SIG_{\hat{CE}}(\hat{X}, C_{\hat{X}})) <$
$Send(Y, \hat{Y}, \hat{X}, ENC_{E_{\hat{X}}}(symkey, HASH(A_{\hat{X}})), ENC_{symkey}(SIG_{\hat{Y}}(\hat{X}, A_{\hat{X}})))$

It has therefore been proven that the certificate request protocol is correct in the sense that the client is communicating with the PCA and the messages the PCA sent where meant for the client.

Last, in order to be sure the certificate retrieval does not violate TLS, it has to be shown that the TLS invariants $\Gamma_{tls,1}$ and $\Gamma_{tls,2}$ are still valid. This is true since the certificate retrieval does not send any TLS *finished* messages, nor does it send *secret* in clear.

The complete zero configuration protocol is therefore correct.

6.7 Interim Conclusion

The TLS TPM extension presented in this chapter provides a possibility to use the AIK credential within a standard authentication protocol – namely TLS. It has been shown that it is not possible to use the certificate directly, however, a good workaround has been found to use the AIK certificate without big changes to the protocol and the network infrastructure. The TLS TPM extension provides a way of provisioning a client with the help of one CA (the PCA) instead of two as proposed with SKAE. Furthermore, by using the TLS extensions mechanism, it provides a way to integrate the new client credentials in a backwards compatible way. Servers that do not support these credentials will simply ignore the extension and cause the handshake to abort.

In addition to the TLS TPM extension, a zero-configuration protocol has been introduced that allows to provision clients during their first connect to a network. Such a scheme is possible with TPMs only since it requires a trusted entity on the client side.

Both protocols have been proved to be correct and secure. The next chapter discusses proof-of-concept implementations of these protocols that will show how easily and transparently the protocols may be implemented.

7

Prototype Implementation

In order to prove the concept of the TPM assisted authentication schemes presented in Chapter 6, two implementations have been done. First of all, a SKAE like approach has been implemented in EAP-TLS and secondly, the zero configuration option has been implemented for TLS.

The prototype implementation of the SKAE like approach has already been started in 2007 within a small testbed at the university. The first tests and evaluations have been done in 2008, followed by a first real world setup and evaluation in 2009.

This chapter discusses the university setup, as well as the implementation details. The real world setup will be shown in Chapter 8.

7.1   The University Testbed

Figure 7.1 shows the testbed deployed at the university in order to implement the very first proof-of-concept prototype.

The client is a Lenovo R61 running Ubuntu Server 8-04 with kernel version 2.6.24-24-server (Ubuntu, 2009). This machine is equipped with a hardware TPM from Atmel (Atmel, 2009). The TPM is compatible with the 1.2 standard (TCG, 2007b) and therefore accessible using the `tpm_tis` kernel module. In order to enable this module, install the kernel sources:

```
apt-get install linux-source-2.6.24
```

and enter the kernel configuration:

```
cd /usr/src/linux
make menuconfig
```

The TPM TIS device driver is hidden under `Device Driver` $\rightarrow$ `Character Devices` $\rightarrow$ `TPM Hardware Support` $\rightarrow$ `TPM Interface Specification 1.2 Interface`. Enable this option (either as a module or fix) in order to be able to access the TPM.

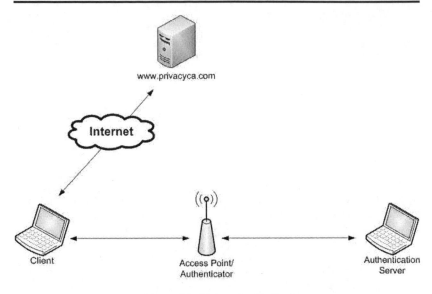

Figure 7.1: University Testbed

The access point is a Linksys WRT54GL running OpenWRT v23 SP2 (OpenWRT, 2009). The authentication server is a very old Dell C500 running Gentoo Linux 2007.0 with kernel 2.6.22.9 (Gentoo, 2009). The only reason why the client is running another Linux distribution than the server was that the client hardware was too new when starting the implementation. Therefore it was decided to install Ubuntu as this Linux distribution has the best hardware support. In general, it does not matter which distribution is used to run the prototype as long as the network interfaces and the TPM are recognized.

Since AIK certificates are needed to test the prototype, AIK certificate requests are sent to www.privacyca.com, which is a PCA setup by a private person for experimental use.

The first proof-of-concept prototype is very similar to the SKAE concept explained in Chapter 6. The *certified key* structure is carried within a X.509 certificate extension and verified by a verification server running on the authentication server.

7.2   The Client Software

The functional layering of the different libraries and software components needed on the client machine is shown in Figure 7.2.

The TPM has already been discussed in Chapter 5. As already mentioned, TPMs compliant with the 1.2 standard are accessible using the TCG PC Client Specific

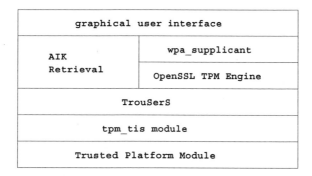

Figure 7.2: Architecture of the Client Software

TPM Interface Specification (TIS). Therefore, the tpm_tis kernel module is used to access the TPM. The layers above the hardware and the device driver are explained in the next sections. Last of all, two possibilities for integrating or splitting these layers into software used by a user are shown.

7.2.1   An Open Source TSS Implementation - TrouSerS

TrouSerS (TrouSerS, 2009) is an open source implementation of the TCG Software Stack (TSS) as specified in (TCG, 2007a). The implementation is mainly driven by IBM developers and therefore of a pretty good quality. TrouSerS is written in C and provides a C API. Since many applications are written in Java nowadays, a team of the OpenTC EU project (OpenTC, 2009) implemented a Java wrapper as well as a full TSS in Java (TU Graz, 2009). However, this thesis is based on TrouSerS since all the applications that had to be modified were written in C.

TrouSerS breaks the TPM specification in four points: The default policy for secrets is TSS_SECRET_MODE_NONE instead of TSS_SECRET_MODE_POPUP. This means by default there is no secret set instead of asking the user to set one. Although that introduces some weaknesses, it is up to the application to assign another policy. Therefore, this is no issue for the implementation.

Second, it is possible to reset the TPM in software only. Usually, this feature should only be possible in the BIOS when showing physical presence. However, the TrouSerS developers wanted to support every TPM, even ones shipped with a machine without TCG enabled BIOS. In case there is a TCG enabled BIOS, the software commands do not cause any action. Since the prototype machine does have a TCG enabled BIOS, this is no issue for this implementation.

Third, the TSS 1.1 implementation of TrouSerS allows to use TSS 1.2 like callbacks. Again, this is no issue for the implementation.

Lastly, the TrouSerS TSS 1.1 implementation allows to control the NULL termination of secrets as specified in TSS 1.2. Summarizing, one can say that TrouSerS does only break the TSS specification with minor impact on applications using TrouSerS. The prototype for TPM assisted authentication will not be affected at all.

TrouSerS can be downloaded from (TrouSerS, 2009) or checked out of the TrouSerS CVS. The latter allows to work with a newer version:

```
cvs -d:pserver:anonymous@trousers.cvs.sourceforge.net:\\
/cvsroot/trousers login
cvs -z3 -d:pserver:anonymous@trousers.cvs.sourceforge.net:\\
/cvsroot/trousers co -P trousers
```

The installation is pretty straightforward:

```
cd trousers
./configure --enable-debug
make
make install
```

The `--enable-debug` option is useful for development environments to be able to track problems down.

As shown in Figure 7.2, the TSS is located between the TPM and applications that make use of the TPM functionality. Under Linux, that extra layer has been implemented as daemon that accesses the TPM using the TPM device driver (e.g. `tpm_tis`) and provides API calls to applications. The daemon is called `tcsd` and may be started either in the background by just typing `tcsd` or in the foreground by giving the `-f` option.

The TrouSerS developers also provide some simple tools to do some TPM operations like taking ownership or printing the version without the need to develop your own application for that. These tools are called `tpm-tools` and are also available in the CVS:

```
cvs -d:pserver:anonymous@trousers.cvs.sourceforge.net:\\
/cvsroot/trousers login
cvs -z3 -d:pserver:anonymous@trousers.cvs.sourceforge.net:\\
/cvsroot/trousers co -P tpm-tools
```

Again, the installation of `tpm-tools` is rather simple:

```
cd tpm-tools
sh ./bootstrap.sh
./configure
make
make install
```

Afterwards, one can start playing with some TPM features, e.g. taking the ownership:

First, start the TSS daemon:

```
tcsd
```

and afterwards try the TPM tools:

```
diufpc272 ~ # tpm_takeownership
Enter owner password:
Confirm password:
Enter SRK password:
Confirm password:
diufpc272 ~ #
```

One may also print the TPM version and the public endorsement key as shown in Listing 7.1.

```
diufpc272 ~ # tpm_version
  TPM 1.2 Version Info:
  Chip Version:        1.2.1.6
  Spec Level:          2
  Errata Revision:     0
  TPM Vendor ID:       NSM
  TPM Version:         01010000
  Manufacturer Info:   4e534d20
diufpc272 ~ # tpm_getpubek
Enter owner password:
Public Endorsement Key:
  Version:    01010000
  Usage:      0x0002 (Unknown)
  Flags:      0x00000000 (!VOLATILE, !MIGRATABLE, !REDIRECTION)
  AuthUsage:  0x00 (Never)
  Algorithm:        0x00000020 (Unknown)
  Encryption Scheme: 0x00000012 (Unknown)
  Signature Scheme:  0x00000010 (Unknown)
  Public Key:
        ce95491f 9dc4660e 3b09a36d b950077a 96a3c36c 1081b71b 8bff994d
            8977d7ab
        b97a97cb 915b1944 f8341d9c 674728b3 c33ddeb2 1010e116 e339be44
            8b738f20
        e90ecd33 a977d5b9 f7680fe5 99a97dab cc637d2e cce2378f 8327293e
            d6a8038e
        aaf2d4f8 bf41d5a5 611e0b06 66cd78b4 5aa7c8a4 70ed1f7a 97955db7
            167d4cd6
        750f6fd5 42d478c1 f75f0005 57465ca6 6a493f21 440d38f0 d96dc9a2
            d0327af3
        0ff4508a 2fccfd54 739ead48 5016ee08 4dd74f9a 9128780c a9e5db5c
            bcf784ee
        93398620 955105da 9a6b5feb 207aba10 6b1ce45f 444961d5 4dd35ca7
            f6fd87f9
        3f43b4ff 61c18d9c f297231c 7def4f26 f197b2e0 bc4c6cdc 045e5d7f
            48ee067d
diufpc272 ~ #
```

Listing 7.1: Examples of tpm-tools

The API provided by TrouSerS defines methods that are almost identical in name and functionality to the TSS specifications, which allows to use the TSS specification (TCG, 2007a) as documentation for the API. Furthermore, every function has a prefix to determine the layer of the TSS shown in Figure 5.1. The prefix `Tspi` that is used for all the methods used by an application provider is short for TCG Service Provider Interface and therefore describes functionality of the TSP layer. The next term defines the location or the subject of the function. The most common subjects are:

- `Tspi_TPM_<name>` - A function located within the TPM.

- `Tspi_TSS_<name>` - A function located within the TSS.

- `Tspi_Context_<name>` - A function dealing with the context of a TPM. A context is a kind of session between an application and a TPM.

- `Tspi_Data_<name>` - This type of function works on data, e.g. it allows to seal data.

- `Tspi_Hash_<name>` - A function working on hashes.

- `Tspi_Key_<name>` - Those are functions dealing with keys like creating and wrapping keys.

This naming scheme enables the application developer to keep a good overview of the individual components and their functionality.

In order for a developer to learn the details about how to use the TrouSerS API, the source code of the `tpm-tools` provides a good starting point. Another good documentation is provided by the TrouSerS testsuite available in the CVS:

```
cvs -d:pserver:anonymous@trousers.cvs.sourceforge.net:\\
/cvsroot/trousers login
cvs -z3 -d:pserver:anonymous@trousers.cvs.sourceforge.net:\\
/cvsroot/trousers co -P testsuite
```

Using the testsuite as an example, almost everything is possible.

In TPM assisted authentication, TrouSerS functionality is accessed directly by the AIK retrieval program and the OpenSSL TPM engine used to integrate the TPM into `wpa_supplicant`. The detailed functions called are explained in the appropriate sections covering the layers.

7.2.2 Obtaining a Client Identity – AIK Retrieval

When starting to implement the prototype of EAP-TLS with the TPM extensions, there already was one Privacy CA (PCA) available for experimental use, called `www.privacyca.com` (Finney, 2009). This PCA provides a REST-style API (Fielding, 2000) and some sample code written in C that is fully compatible with TrouSerS. However, at the moment, the source code for this PCA has not been released for private deployments. This is different for the Java version of a PCA, implemented by the team of the OpenTC EU project (TU Graz, 2009). The Java PCA uses the XML Key Management Protocol XKMS (W3C, 2009) to communicate between client and PCA, which is the protocol recommended by the TCG for credential management. However, the Java PCA is not yet fully compatible with C clients. Furthermore, it was released after the prototype implementation had started. Therefore, the prototype uses www.privacyca.com so far.

www.privacyca.com provides a sample code for AIK retrieval, which has been used as a starting point on the client side. As mentioned in Chapter 5, three certificates are needed to request an AIK:

1. The endorsement credential,

2. the platform credential, and

3. the conformance credential.

So far, no manufacturer delivers these three certificates together. Infineon is the only one that delivers at least the endorsement credential. Therefore, the AIK retrieval starts with creating a fake endorsement credential shown in Listing 7.2 while the other credentials are ignored at the moment.

```
/* code provided by www.privacyca.com */
static TSS_RESULT
makeEKCert(TSS_HCONTEXT hContext, TSS_HTPM hTPM, UINT32 *pCertLen, BYTE
    **pCert)
{
        TSS_RESULT      result;
        TSS_HKEY        hPubek;
        UINT32          modulusLen;
        BYTE            *modulus;

        result = Tspi_TPM_GetPubEndorsementKey (hTPM, TRUE, NULL, &
            hPubek);
        if (result != TSS_SUCCESS)
                return result;
        result = Tspi_GetAttribData (hPubek, TSS_TSPATTRIB_RSAKEY_INFO,
                TSS_TSPATTRIB_KEYINFO_RSA_MODULUS, &modulusLen, &
                    modulus);
        Tspi_Context_CloseObject (hContext, hPubek);
        if (result != TSS_SUCCESS)
                return result;
        if (modulusLen != 256) {
                Tspi_Context_FreeMemory (hContext, modulus);
                return TSS_E_FAIL;
        }
        *pCertLen = sizeof(fakeEKCert);
        *pCert = malloc (*pCertLen);
        memcpy (*pCert, fakeEKCert, *pCertLen);
        memcpy (*pCert + 0xc6, modulus, modulusLen);
        Tspi_Context_FreeMemory (hContext, modulus);
```

```
      return TSS_SUCCESS ;
}
```

Listing 7.2: Creating a Fake Endorsement Credential

Obviously, this method is only needed for non-Infineon TPMs. In order to cover the different security levels resulting from the difference between real endorsement credentials and fake credentials, `www.privacyca.com` defines three certification levels:

1. Level 0 - Certificates with this level are for testing purposes only, since they do not need platform credentials and allow to use faked endorsement credentials. These certificates are used in the prototype.

2. Level 1 - These certificates are issued if an endorsement credential of a known TPM manufacturer was sent within the certificate request.

3. Level 2 - This is the highest level, which is assigned to certificates that use endorsement and platform credentials of known manufacturers.

After having created the fake endorsement credential, the process of retrieving a new AIK may start. The implementation follows the algorithm discussed in Chapter 5, Section 5.3.5. It starts with calling `Tspi_TSS_CollateIdentityRequest`, which calls `TPM_MakeIdentity` internally and collects all the information necessary to be sent to `www.privacyca.com`. This includes the fake endorsement credential. Afterwards, the request is transmitted to `www.privacyca.com`. That is done using the `curl` library (cURL, 2009). After having received the reply from the PCA, the certificate is decrypted and verified by the TPM by calling `Tspi_TPM_ActivateIdentity` which internally recovers the key. As already mentioned, the AIK retrieval source code has been provided by `www.privacyca.com`.

```
Tspi_Context_CreateObject(con,TSS_OBJECT_TYPE_RSAKEY ,
                          TSS_KEY_TYPE_SIGNING | TSS_KEY_SIZE_2048 |
                          TSS_KEY_NOT_MIGRATABLE |
                              TSS_KEY_AUTHORIZATION ,
                          &hKey) ;

Tspi_SetAttribUint32(hKey,TSS_TSPATTRIB_KEY_INFO ,
                     TSS_TSPATTRIB_KEYINFO_SIGSCHEME ,
                     TSS_SS_RSASSAPKCS1V15_DER) ;
```

Listing 7.3: Creating a Key with the TSS_SS_RSASSAPKCS1V15_DER Signing Scheme

Now that the client has a valid AIK credential, a *certified key* has to be created. The key needs to have a signing scheme of **TSS_SS_RSASSAPKCS1V15_DER** as mentioned in Chapter 5. As shown in Listing 7.3, one needs to create a key object first with the properties of being a signing key (TSS_KEY_TYPE_SIGNING), having a key length of 2048 bit (TSS_KEY_SIZE_2048), and being non-migratable (TSS_KEY_NOT_MIGRATABLE). Furthermore, the key needs authorization, which is indicated by TSS_KEY_AUTHORIZATION. Afterwards, the signing scheme needs to be set to TSS_SS_RSASSAPKCS1V15_DER needed for TLS. That is done using Tspi_SetAttribUint32.

Afterwards, the new key hKey needs to be signed by the AIK hIdent:

```
Tspi_Key_CertifyKey(hKey,hIdent,&keyVal);
```

The TPM_CERTIFY_INFO structure will be written to keyVal:

```
TCPA_CERTIFY_INFO struct:
    version:        1100
    keyUsage:       10
    keyFlags:       0
    authDataUsage:  1
    algorithmParams:
       ID:          1
       encScheme:   1
       sigScheme:   3
       parmSize:    12
       parms:       008000020000
    pubkeyDigest:   8aca5e50c1d2776c4a2b25a6bce78d2584f3c7
    nonce:          1832e2b71832e2b7d6f0b27446281a1b2c4d7eb
```

Instead of using the SKAE extension directly – which was not possible due to missing support in TLS libraries – self-defined extensions have been used that carry the TPM_CERTIFY_INFO as well as the signature itself:

```
struct entry ext_entries[22] =
{
  {"basicConstraints","CA:FALSE"},
  {"authorityKeyIdentifier","keyid,issuer:always"},
  {"tpmCert","true"},
  {"version-major",""},
  {"version-minor",""},
  {"version-revMajor",""},
  {"version-revMinor",""},
  {"keyUsage",""},
  {"keyFlags",""},
  {"authDataUsage",""},
  {"algorithmID",""},
  {"encScheme",""},
  {"sigScheme",""},
  {"parmSize",""},
  {"parms",""},
```

```
  {"pubkeyDigest",""},
  {"nonce",""},
  {"parentPCRStatus",""},
  {"PCRInfoSize",""},
  {"PCRInfo",""},
  {"tpmSigLen",""},
  {"tpmSig",""}
};
```

This certificate will be self-signed and used for client authentication in TLS.

7.2.3   TPM Integration Into Common TLS Libraries

The most common TLS libraries under Linux are OpenSSL (OpenSSL, 2009) and GnuTLS (GnuTLS, 2009). Both libraries provide interfaces for cryptographical tokens, but both interfaces are very different from each other. In addition to the library-specific interfaces, there is a PKCS#11 interface as well. This section discusses all three possible ways to use the TPM in TLS libraries and ends with a short conclusion.

The OpenSSL TPM Engine

From OpenSSL version 0.9.6 on, there was a new concept called OpenSSL Engine (Messier *et al.*, 2002). In general, engines allow to integrate for instance alternative RSA implementations. Such alternative implementations may be done using acceleration hardware or hardware tokens like smart cards to be used with OpenSSL. IBM has released an OpenSSL engine for the TPM in 2007 (K.Yoder, 2009), which has been used in a slightly modified version for this prototype.

The OpenSSL TPM engine can be used to delegate private key operations to the TPM. Like this the private keys is never available in software. In the original TPM engine, keys are stored in key blobs and loaded using the `Tspi_Context_LoadKeyBy Blob`. Since the prototype stores the keys non-volatile inside the TPM, they can be loaded using their Universal Unique ID (UUID) using `Tspi_Context_LoadKeyByUUID`. Therefore, in order to use the OpenSSL TPM engine with the prototype, the first method has been replaced with the latter.

The details about how to call the OpenSSL engine within an application are explained in the next section.

GnuTLS Callbacks

GnuTLS (GnuTLS, 2009) is another open source TLS library that even supports TLS 1.2 already. Therefore, some tests were also done using the GnuTLS library. GnuTLS does not provide a feature such as engines to integrate hardware tokens, but it provides a callback function `gnutls_sign_callback_set` to integrate customized signing functions. This callback can also be used for integrating signing functionality of hardware tokens.

Among others, the callback gets the hash to sign as parameter and has to return the signature.

```
int gnutls_tpm_sign (gnutls_session_t session,
        void *userdata,
        gnutls_certificate_type_t cert_type,
        const gnutls_datum_t * cert,
        const gnutls_datum_t * hash,
        gnutls_datum_t * signature) {

    TSS_RESULT result;
    TSS_HKEY hKey;
    TSS_HHASH hHash;
    TSS_UUID uuid;
    int i;

    // Create Context
    result = Tspi_Context_Create(&hContext);
    handleResult("Tspi_Context_Create", result);

    // Connect Context
    result = Tspi_Context_Connect(hContext, NULL);
    handleResult("Tspi_Context_Connect", result);

    // Create hash object
    result = Tspi_Context_CreateObject (hContext, TSS_OBJECT_TYPE_HASH,
        TSS_HASH_SHA1, &hHash);
    handleResult("Tspi_Context_CreateObject", result);

    // Set digest
    result = Tspi_Hash_SetHashValue(hHash, hash->size, hash->data);
    handleResult("Tspi_Hash_SetHashValue", result);

    read_uuid_from_file(uuidfile,&uuid);

    result = Tspi_Context_LoadKeyByUUID(hContext, TSS_PS_TYPE_SYSTEM,
        uuid, &hKey);\
    handleResult("Tspi_Context_LoadKeyByUUID", result);

    // Sign hash
    result = Tspi_Hash_Sign (hHash, hKey, &(signature->size), &(signature
        ->data));
    handleResult("Tspi_Hash_Sign", result);

    Tspi_Context_Close (hContext);
}
```

Listing 7.4: TPM Sign Callback in GnuTLS

Listing 7.4 shows how to use the callback for integrating the TPM into GnuTLS. The hash that has been passed to the callback needs to be converted into the TSS_OBJECT_TYPE_HASH format first. That is done by creating a new

TSS_OBJECT_TYPE
_HASH object, which is then initialized with the hash value in Tspi_Hash_SetHash
Value. The UUID of the key to be used for signing the hash has been stored in a file
and has to be read before loading the key. Afterwards, it will be loaded and used to
sign the hash.

Next, in order to tell GnuTLS to use the callback method, one needs to set a
NULL private key when initializing GnuTLS:

```
gnutls_certificate_set_x509_key_mem(xcred,
                                    CERTFILE,
                                    NULL,
                                    GNUTLS_X509_FMT_PEM);
```

Lastly, GnuTLS needs to know about the exact callback:

```
gnutls_sign_callback_set(session, gnutls_tpm_sign, NULL);
```

Afterwards, GnuTLS will pass all hashes that need to be signed during the TLS
handshake to gnutls_tpm_sign that uses the TPM for signing then.

The PKCS#11 Interface for the TPM

PKCS#11 is short for Public Key Cryptography Standard number 11 (RSA, 2009)
and describes an interface to access cryptographic tokens like smart cards or cryptographic accelerators. Tokens are organized in slots that may be available at application run time. Applications that support PKCS#11 tokens query all of the slots to
find the token most suitable for the functionality needed. A PKCS#11 token knows
two passwords:

1. the security officer (SO) PIN that is used for administration purposes, and

2. the user PIN used to access the token's data.

In general, the functionality of TSS and a PKCS#11 token is quite similar.
Both provide storage for certificates, keys, and data as well as some cryptographic
functions like asymmetric cryptography.

TrouSerS provides an interface for PKCS#11. In order to use it, install TrouSerS
first as mentioned in Section 7.2.1. Afterwards, install openCryptoki (openCryptoki,
2009):

```
cvs -d:pserver:anonymous@opencryptoki.cvs.sourceforge.net:\\
/cvsroot/opencryptoki login
cvs -z3 -d:pserver:anonymous@opencryptoki.cvs.sourceforge.net:\\
/cvsroot/opencryptoki co -P opencryptoki
```

Now, install it the usual way:

```
sh bootstrap.sh
./configure
make
make install
```

Last, install tpm-tools as described in Section 7.2.1.

In order to use the PKCS#11 interface for the TPM, the SRK password needs to be set to NULL. This can be done using either tpm_takeownership if the TPM does not have an owner yet, or tpm_changeownerauth otherwise. In order to set the SRK password to NULL, hit return when asked for the password.

Start the PKCS#11 services to access the TPM and add your local user to the pkcs11 group:

```
usermod -a -G pkcs11 latze
/usr/local/sbin/pkcs11_startup
/etc/init.d/pkcsslotd start
```

Now, let openCryptoki list the tokens available on the system:

```
basisk:~# pkcsconf -t
Token #0 Info:
      Label: IBM OS PKCS#11
      Manufacturer: IBM Corp.
      Model: IBM SoftTok
      Serial Number: 123
      Flags: 0x980445 (RNG|LOGIN_REQUIRED|CLOCK_ON_TOKEN|
                       TOKEN_INITIALIZED|
                       USER_PIN_TO_BE_CHANGED|SO_PIN_COUNT_LOW|
                       SO_PIN_TO_BE_CHANGED)
      Sessions: -1/-1
      R/W Sessions: -1/-1
      PIN Length: 4-8
      Public Memory: 0xFFFFFFFF/0xFFFFFFFF
      Private Memory: 0xFFFFFFFF/0xFFFFFFFF
      Hardware Version: 1.0
      Firmware Version: 1.0
      Time: 04:45:30 PM
```

The TPM token is already available, but there are some problems indicated by the flags, e.g. USER_PIN_TO_BE_CHANGED and SO_PIN_TO_BE_CHANGED. Therefore, execute the first command to change the SO PIN and the second to change the user PIN:

```
pkcsconf -c 0 -P
pkcsconf -c 0 -u
```

The default SO PIN is 87654321, which is important to know for executing the first command. Listing the token now shows that some flags have disappeared:

```
basisk:~# pkcsconf -t
Token #0 Info:
      Label: tpm
      Manufacturer: IBM Corp.
      Model: IBM SoftTok
      Serial Number: 123
      Flags: 0x44D (RNG|LOGIN_REQUIRED|USER_PIN_INITIALIZED|
                    CLOCK_ON_TOKEN|TOKEN_INITIALIZED)
      Sessions: -1/-1
      R/W Sessions: -1/-1
      PIN Length: 4-8
      Public Memory: 0xFFFFFFFF/0xFFFFFFFF
      Private Memory: 0xFFFFFFFF/0xFFFFFFFF
      Hardware Version: 1.0
      Firmware Version: 1.0
      Time: 04:50:14 PM
```

The token is now ready to be used in applications using the PKCS#11 functions. (Käser, 2010) shows how to use the PKCS#11 TPM with Firefox to encrypt the stored passwords.

Since the TPM has not been designed to meet the PKCS#11 interface, some limitations exist when using the PKCS#11 TPM interface. PKCS#11 allows to set RSA padding types at signing or encryption time, which means they can change with every operation. However, TPM keys have a fixed RSA padding scheme once they are created. Furthermore, PKCS#11 allows to create keys for signing and encryption, which is not desired for TPM keys. The only key type in TPMs that allows both are legacy keys. In order to cover most of the PKCS#11 applications, TPM keys in openCryptoki are by default of the type TSS_KEY_TYPE_LEGACY with the TSS_ES_RSAESPKCSV15 encryption scheme and the TSS_SS_RSASSAPKCS1V15_DER signing scheme. As mentioned in Chapter 5, the use of legacy keys is not recommended due to possible security problems, but at the moment, there is no better solution for using TPM keys in PKCS#11.

Another problem is the administration of the TPM. Especially the setup, such as taking ownership cannot be done in PKCS#11, as already shown in the little example above. Furthermore, there are additional administration routines like setting the SO and user PIN that cannot be done via TSS calls, which is why they have to be done after setting up the TPM using the TSS calls. Since PKCS#11 users cannot be forced to be familiar with the TPM, asking them for SRK password when loading keys would cause huge confusion. Therefore, the SRK has to be set to NULL in order for openCryptoki to be able to use a NULL password internally. If using the NULL password, there is no need to bother the user anymore.

Summarizing, it is possible to access the TPM using PKCS#11 libraries like openCryptoki but not without limitations and weaknesses.

Interim Conclusion

As shown above, there are elegant ways to integrate the TPM into popular open source TLS libraries like OpenSSL and GnuTLS. It is even possible to use standard PKCS#11 interfaces in order to work with the TPM. However, since the TPM PKCS#11 interface introduces weaknesses by using legacy keys and setting the SRK password to NULL, it has been decided not to use that approach, but to use either the OpenSSL engine or the GnuTLS callback.

The OpenSSL engine is a very powerful concept providing most of the TPM functionality to OpenSSL based applications. In contrast, GnuTLS does not provide an abstraction of hardware tokens, but only allows for certain callbacks that may use hardware tokens. However, since EAP-TLS with the TPM extensions requires the TPM only during the TLS handshake, the GnuTLS callback would be sufficient. Furthermore, GnuTLS provides better documentation and code samples for developers, which is why GnuTLS has been used to implement the TLS-only proof of concept prototypes.

The OpenSSL engine concept allows for an easier integration into applications like wpa_supplicant, as shown in Section 7.2.4. This is due to the fact that the use of a new OpenSSL engine is only a configuration option. Using the GnuTLS callback would require bigger changes to the application's source code. Therefore, the OpenSSL engine has been used to show the integration of the TPM assisted authentication into other applications such as EAP.

7.2.4 An Open Source Peer - wpa_supplicant

Under Linux, there are several Open Source WLAN clients such as XSupplicant (Open1X, 2009) and wpa_supplicant (Malinen, 2009). Since the latter is the one used in common distributions like Ubuntu (Ubuntu, 2009), it has been decided to use wpa_supplicant for the proof of concept prototype. wpa_supplicant does provide EAP authentication, as well as WEP and WPA/ WPA2.

wpa_supplicant did already provide OpenSSL engine support, although some bugs needed to be fixed first in order to use the engine in EAP tunneling methods as well.

In order to integrate the TPM engine itself into wpa_supplicant, it had to be added to the TLS related files, as well as to the configuration file.

Besides some variables, the first function needed to use the OpenSSL TPM engine is the one to load the engine:

```
static int tls_engine_load_dynamic_tpm(const char *tpm_so_path)
{
  char *engine_id = "tpm";
  const char *pre_cmd[] = {
    "SO_PATH", NULL /* tpm_so_path */,
    "ID", NULL /* engine_id */,
    "LIST_ADD", "1",
    "LOAD", NULL,
    NULL, NULL
```

```
};
if (!tpm_so_path)
   return 0;

pre_cmd[1] = tpm_so_path;
pre_cmd[3] = engine_id;

wpa_printf(MSG_DEBUG, "ENGINE: Loading TPM Engine from %s",
   tpm_so_path);

return tls_engine_load_dynamic_generic(pre_cmd, NULL, engine_id);
}
```

This function takes the path to the engine's .so file specified in wpa_supplicant's configuration file and the specific engine ID, which is "tpm" in our case, to load the engine.

Second, a new configuration file option had to be defined in order to point to the path where the engine's .so file resides:

```
static int
wpa_config_process_tpm_engine_path(struct wpa_config *config,
      char *pos)
{
  os_free(config->tpm_engine_path);
  config->tpm_engine_path = os_strdup(pos);
  wpa_printf(MSG_DEBUG, "tpm_engine_path='%s'",
     config->tpm_engine_path);
  return 0;
}
```

This is all t6hat is necessary to include a new OpenSSL engine into wpa_supplicant. The remaining engine functionality is generic and does not need to be adapted for TPM engines. The following listing shows an example configuration file that configures wpa_supplicant to use the TPM engine in EAP-TLS:

```
ctrl_interface=/var/run/wpa_supplicant

eapol_version=2
ap_scan=1
fast_reauth=1

tpm_engine_path=/usr/local/lib/openssl/engines/libtpm.so

network={
        ssid="DEV-MOBILE-EAPSIM"
        scan_ssid=0
        key_mgmt=IEEE8021X
```

```
            eap=TLS
            identity="sis@sc-eaptpm.ch"
# EAP-TLS with TPM
            ca_cert="/home/latze/pwlan/cert/cacert.pem"
            client_cert="/home/latze/impl/basisk-eap.pem"
            engine=1
            engine_id="tpm"
            key_id="3"
            pin="PASSWORD"


}
```

The configuration file starts with the standard declarations (ctrl_interface etc) and has the standard structure. In order to be able to load the OpenSSL TPM engine, wpa_supplicant needs to find the .so file generated when compiling the engine:

```
tpm_engine_path=/usr/local/lib/openssl/engines/libtpm.so
```

The client wants to use EAP-TLS with WEP. Furthermore, it announces its identity in order for the NAS to know which authentication server to use:

```
ssid="DEV-MOBILE-EAPSIM"
scan_ssid=0
key_mgmt=IEEE8021X
eap=TLS
identity="sis@sc-eaptpm.ch"
```

Afterwards, the certificates are specified including the TPM:

```
ca_cert="/home/latze/pwlan/cert/cacert.pem"
client_cert="/home/latze/impl/basisk-eap.pem"
engine=1
engine_id="tpm"
key_id="3"
pin="PASSWORD"
```

pin is used as owner and SRK password at the same time in the prototype. In order to distinguish those two, a new configuration file option has to be added. Since this does not influence the authentication itself, it has not been implemented yet. key_id should carry the complete UUID of a key, but for simplicity reasons, the prototype assumes the first 15 bytes to be zero and reads the last byte out of key_id. client_cert specifies the *certified key* certificate created in Section 7.2.2. The AIK certificate itself is not transmitted in the first prototype. It is assumed that there is a central storage for AIK certificates somewhere in the network like it is assumed in SKAE (The Trusted Computing Group, 2005).

7.2.5   The User Interface - Standalone Software vs. Webportal

During the work on the prototype, two types of user interfaces have been implemented: One for dummy users that provides a standalone solution, and one for advanced users that needs some interaction.

Standalone Software

The standalone software is perfectly suited to inexperienced users since it simplifies the configuration. The prototype has been implemented using Tcl/Tk (Tcl/Tk, 2009), which does probably not lead to the most beautiful results. However, the software has been implemented as proof of concept and would need a re-implementation for use as a product anyway.

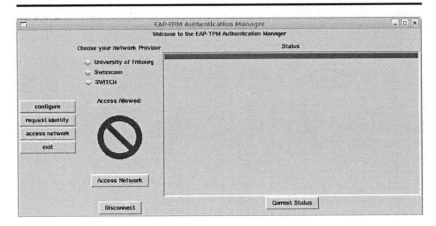

Figure 7.3: Start Screen

Figure 7.3 shows the start screen of the tool. Most of the time, users will have identities for the appropriate networks already, so they just need to choose their provider and connect as shown in Figure 7.4.

The status field on the right side shows the connection status, which can be SCANNING, CONNECTING, AUTHENTICATING, or DISCONNECTED.

In case a user tries to access a network she does not have an identity for, the application shows a red "forbidden" sign (see Figure 7.5) and allows the user to request a new identity.

Figure 7.5 shows the GUI for requesting a new identity. The user chooses the provider that operates the network she wants to access. The status field will show messages like `connecting` or `downloading credentials`. After having completed the request, the user might need to configure the network as shown in Figure 7.6.

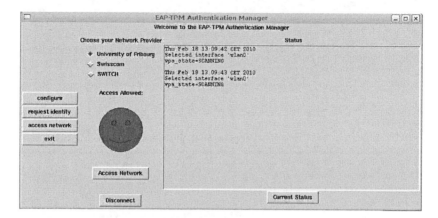

Figure 7.4: Connecting

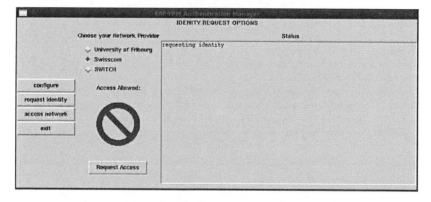

Figure 7.5: Requesting a New Identity

Network configuration in this client is pretty simple. All the user needs to know is the network ID (the SSID), her user ID (something like `carolin.latze@unifr.ch`) and her TPM password (at the moment the same for owner and SRK).

All the complexity of configuring and calling wpa_supplicant and an AIK retrieval tool are hidden behind the GUI. Therefore, the standalone software is a good solution for inexperienced users. However, experienced users may want to configure their software themselves. Furthermore, self-configured software is much cheaper for the operator, which is why a webportal has been implemented too.

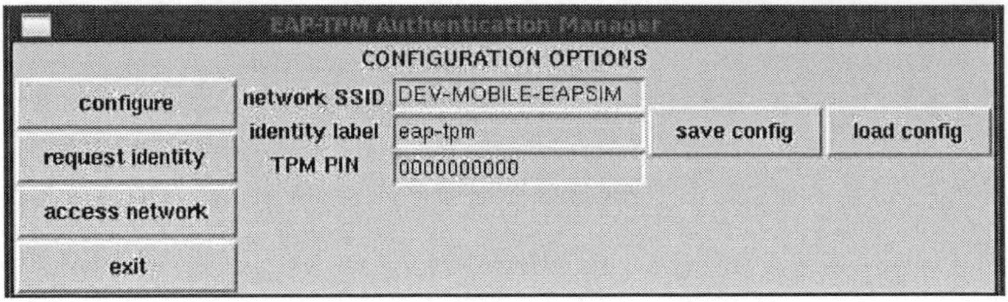

Figure 7.6: Configuring the Client

Webportal

The standalone software client proposed in Section 7.2.5 can be very useful for inexperienced users who are not able to configure their system by themselves. Furthermore, it requires a user to have an install CD-ROM including that client. A webportal that allows to request a new identity without having to install a software and that provides a sample configuration for the user's WLAN client solves some of the problems. It allows to connect to a network without the need to install a special software client first. However, it requires the user to be able to configure her operating system's WLAN client without much support (except for a how-to on the page). Furthermore, there needs to be a way to identify the user in order to be able to bind an identity to a user. That can be done either by asking the user for her credit card number or by asking her for her mobile or fixnet phone number. The latter has been implemented in the proof of concept portal.

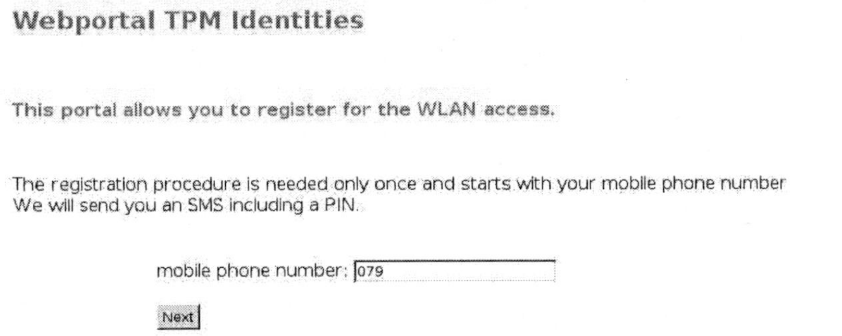

Webportal TPM Identities

This portal allows you to register for the WLAN access.

The registration procedure is needed only once and starts with your mobile phone number
We will send you an SMS including a PIN.

mobile phone number: 079

Next

Figure 7.7: Webportal Entry Page

Figure 7.7 shows the entry page of the webportal. On the first page, the user is asked to give her mobile phone number, which allows to authenticate a user. In order to ensure that the user did not input another one's phone number, the user will receive an SMS including a 4 digit PIN number. The next page asks the user for that PIN before she is able to proceed (see Figure 7.8).

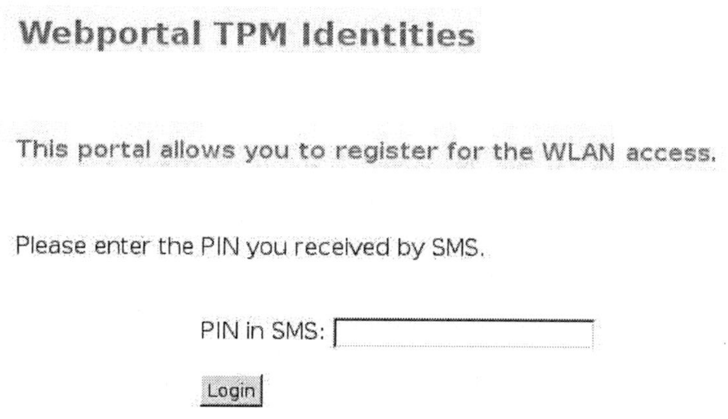

Webportal TPM Identities

This portal allows you to register for the WLAN access.

Please enter the PIN you received by SMS.

PIN in SMS: [   ]

[Login]

Figure 7.8: Webportal Asking for the PIN Sent by SMS

After that step, one can be sure that the user gave the correct phone number. Next, she has to choose whether she already has an identity that she wants to register for that phone number or not. In case she has an identity, he will be asked to upload the appropriate pem-file. This is the final step before she gets the configuration parameters (e.g. an example configuration file) for her WLAN client. The server maps the identity to the mobile phone number for accounting purposes.

In case the user does not have a usable identity yet, she is asked to download a program that generates a new identity request. Afterwards, the user is asked to upload that request and wait for the reply. When the reply arrives, it is registered with the user's mobile phone number and the user is able to download the new identity. Finally, she gets a configuration manual for her WLAN client.

7.2.6 Interim Conclusion

This section presented two different possibilities for real world client side deployments. The first one is a standalone client solution that integrates the identity management as well as the WLAN authentication client. Such a solution requires the user to install a client prior to the first connect. Apart from that, it is a very user-friendly setup since the user gets a nice GUI and does not need to know anything about the underlying architecture and dependencies. However, advanced users might prefer to use their standard WLAN client. Furthermore, there will be roaming users who want to get access for one day without the need to install software first. In order to cover these use cases, a webportal has been implemented that allows for identity management and WLAN configuration without additional software. Both implementations have a right to exist since they are made for different use cases.

7.3   The Server Software

The authentication server runs FreeRADIUS (DeKok, 2009a), which is an open source RADIUS server. Since FreeRADIUS is widely deployed (according to (DeKok, 2009a), it is the most widely deployed RADIUS server) and provides a good community support, it was the first choice for the prototype.

Because a SKAE like approach has been implemented, the verification of the client certificates had to be extended. In order to keep the modifications of FreeRADIUS itself small, a verification service has been implemented that is used by FreeRADIUS to verify the client certificates.

7.3.1   An Open Source RADIUS Server - FreeRADIUS

FreeRADIUS supports a wide range of EAP methods for authentication including EAP-TLS (Simon *et al.*, 2008), EAP-SIM (Haverinen & Salowey, 2006), and EAP-TTLS (Funk & Blake-Wilson, 2004). Since the prototype does not change the authentication protocol itself, but only the certificate handling, the EAP-TLS module needed only slight modifications.

The only file modified is `rlm_eap_tls.c`. The modifications are only needed for clients using *certified key* certificates, which is why FreeRADIUS will always try to verify the client certificate using standard OpenSSL calls first. In case the verification fails, the server checks whether it got a *certified key* certificate which carries a special issuer:

```
issuer[sizeof(issuer) - 1] = '\0';
if (strcmp(issuer,"/CN=TPM-basisk")==0)
...
```

In the prototype, the issuer is set to `CN=TPM-basisk` because the hostname of the client is basisk. Such a setup is only suitable for a proof of concept prototype. As the final product will use the TLS TPM extensions proposed in Chapter 6, there will be no need for the RADIUS server to distinguish certificates that way. In case the extension message is sent by the client, the server already knows that it has to verify the certificate in another way.

All FreeRADIUS now does with the *certified key* certificate is to sent its extensions to the verification service as shown in Listing 7.5.

```
int do_client_loop(SSL *ssl, X509 *cert)
{
   int err;
```

```
int extcount;
unsigned char result[3];

if((extcount=X509_get_ext_count(cert)) > 0)
{
    int i,j;
    fprintf(stdout,"This certificate has %d extension(s)\n",extcount);
    for(i=0;i<extcount;i++)
    {
        X509_EXTENSION *ext;
        const unsigned char *extstr;
        ASN1_OCTET_STRING *os;
        int len;

        ext=X509_get_ext(cert,i);
        os=X509_EXTENSION_get_data(ext);
        len=ASN1_STRING_length(os);
        extstr=ASN1_STRING_data(os);
        err=SSL_write(ssl,extstr,len);
        fprintf(stdout,"SENT (len=%d) : %s\n",len,extstr);
        if(i==14)
        {
            int k;
            fprintf(stdout,"SENT: ");
            for (k=0;k<len;k++) fprintf(stdout,"%x",extstr[k]);
            fprintf(stdout,"\n");
        }
        if(i==21)
        {
            int k;
            fprintf(stdout,"SENT: ");
            for (k=0;k<len;k++) fprintf(stdout,"%x",extstr[k]);
            fprintf(stdout,"\n");
        }
    }
}
memset(result,0,3*sizeof(char));
err=SSL_read(ssl,result,3);
if(err<=0) fprintf(stdout,"ERROR: SSL_read failed\n");
if(strcmp(result,"OK")==0)
{
    fprintf(stdout,"\nINFO: certificate correct\n");
    return 1;
}
else
{
    fprintf(stdout,"\nINFO: certificate invalid (%s)\n",result);
    return 0;
}
}
```

Listing 7.5: FreeRADIUS Client for the Verification Service

Since the extensions are sent as strings in the first prototype, some weird conversions are needed, which will be hidden or disappear in the final product.

In order to be able to communicate with the verification service in a secure way, TLS is used. The FreeRADIUS server already has a TLS certificate since it has to authenticate itself to the client.

7.3.2   The Verification Service

As already mentioned, the verification service is only needed in the first proof-of-concept prototype in order to able to be handle the SKAE like client certificates. The verification service needs to have a certificate in order to be able to authenticate mutually with the FreeRADIUS server. This certificate may be signed by the authentication server or by any CA.

In order to be able to verify the SKAE like extensions, the verification service has to reconstruct the `TPM_CERTIFY_INFO` structure. That is done dependent on the extension number, for instance for extension i=3:

```
switch (i)
 {
    case 3:
      str=(char*)malloc((strlen(trim(buf))+1)*sizeof(char));
      sprintf(str,"%s",trim(buf));
      str[strlen(trim(buf))]='\0';
      tpmcert.version.major=str[0];
      free(str);
      break;
 ...
```

where `tpmcert` is the `TPM_CERTIFY_INFO` structure. The last extension includes the signature of the `TPM_CERTIFY_INFO` done with the client's AIK certificate. In order to be able to verify that signature, the verification service needs to have access to the AIK certificates of the clients. That could be ensured by storing all the AIK certificates at the PCA with an API for the verification service. Another possibility is using the PCA itself to run the verification service, which is the setup chosen for the prototype. Therefore, the verification service is able to find the correct AIK certificate and verify the signature. In case the signatures match, the verification service signals a SUCCESS message to the FreeRADIUS server, whereas FAILURE is sent in case the signatures do not match.

7.3.3   Interim Conclusion

The prototype implementation shows the complexity of the SKAE approach, since there needs to be a certificate store somewhere that holds the AIK certificates. That was easy to implement in the test network, but will cause problems in real world setups. However, it is already obvious that the slight changes to TLS are rather easy to implement and are also transparent to the upper layers. It has therefore been shown that it is possible to implement an authentication protocol like that with acceptable effort.

7.4 The Zero Configuration Protocol

In order to be able to evaluate the usability of the zero-configuration option presented in Section 6.5, a simple proof-of-concept prototype has been prepared. The prototype is based on a RESTful proxy Certificate Authority (CA) that relays the client's certificate request to the desired PCA and the GnuTLS library. It has been decided to use GnuTLS for that prototype since this library provides some nice callbacks that allow for an easy intervention of the TLS handshake.

This section starts with a short architectural overview, goes on with the technical details and ends with a short conclusion.

7.4.1 Zero Configuration Prototype Architecture

Figure 7.9 gives an overview of the architecture chosen for the prototype.

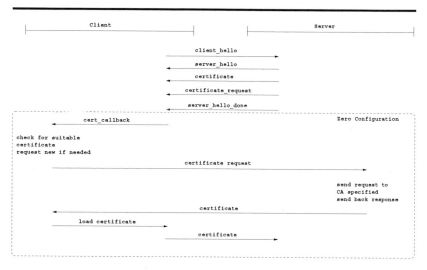

Figure 7.9: Architecture Overview Zero Configuration Prototype

On the client as well as on the server, two protocols are running:

1. the TLS protocol, and

2. the certificate request protocol.

The TLS handshake will start as specified in (Dierks & Rescorla, 2008) until the server sends the `certificate_request` message including the CAs it accepts. Afterwards, a callback is called that allows to check whether any of the certificates available on the client has been signed by one of those CAs. If an appropriate certificate has been found, the client loads the certificate and finishes the handshake. In case there is no such certificate, the client prepares a request and sends it to the server that forwards it to the certificate authority the client specified. The server provides a REST interface to send the requests and retrieve the responses (Fielding, 2000). After having received the response, which includes the new certificate, the client loads the certificate and goes on with the handshake.

7.4.2   A RESTful Web Interface

REST is short for representational state transfer and has been specified by (Fielding, 2000). It is an architectural style that allows to design scalable and easy to implement setups. REST is based on HTTP which allows to concentrate on the service to implement without the need to think about problems like error handling because they have already been solved.

RESTful applications provide resources that are identified by URIs. In the zero-configuration prototype, there is only one resource that takes the client's certificate request as input and outputs the signed certificate:

`http://SERVER/proxyCA.php`

In general, RESTful applications can provide four different methods:

1. `POST`: creates a new resource

2. `GET`: retrieves a representation of a resource

3. `PUT`: updates a resource

4. `DELETE`: deletes a resource

The zero-configuration prototype uses the `POST` method to submit the certificate request and retrieve the response.

7.4.3   The ProxyCA

As mentioned above, the ProxyCA server uses a REST interface for applications. It runs on `apache2` with `php5`, which can be installed under Ubuntu using `apt-get install apache2 php5`.

```php
$CLIENTREQ="zero-request.pem";
$CLIENTCERT="zero-cert.pem";
$CACERT  = "ca.pem";
$CAKEY  = "ca-key.pem";

$target_path="./";
$target_path = $target_path . basename($_FILES['uploadedfile']['name'])
    ;

if(move_uploaded_file($_FILES['uploadedfile']['tmp_name'], $target_path
    )) {
```

```
$cmd="certtool —generate-certificate —load-request ".$CLIENTREQ."
    —outfile ".$CLIENTCERT." —load-ca-certificate ".$CACERT." —load
    -ca-privkey ".$CAKEY." —template certtool.cfg";
system($cmd);
header('Content-type: application/octet-stream');
header('Content-Disposition: attachment; filename="zero-cert.pem"');
readfile('zero-cert.pem');
} else{
echo "There was an error uploading the file, please try again!";
}
```

Listing 7.6: ProxyCA Source Code

Listing 7.6 shows the source code of the ProxyCA used in the prototype. It has been implemented in PHP and looks exactly the same as a script called after a HTML form submit. The script is able to receive a file using the POST method, which should be the client's certificate request. In a real-world setup assumed in Section 6.5, the ProxyCA might forward that request to the CA specified by the client. However, it is also possible that the network provider the client wants to authenticate to provides its own CA and does therefore sign the client's request itself. This has been implemented in the proof-of-concept. The server is a CA itself and is therefore able to sign the client's request using applications like certtool. Last of all, the server provides the new certificate zero-cert.pem to the client.

7.4.4 The TLS Server

The server is basically a standard TLS server that accepts client connections and requests mutual authentication. Furthermore, it sends the client a list of acceptable certificate authorities, which is done using the gnutls_certificate_server_set_request method. That method requests a certificate from the client and sends acceptable certificate issuers set by gnutls_certificate_set_x509_trust_file.

7.4.5 The Client

The zero-configuration client is implemented as a normal TLS client except that it does not set a certificate right from the beginning. It rather uses a callback that is called after the server has sent the certificate request. GnuTLS allows to set those callbacks using gnutls_certificate_client_set_retrieve_function and passes all the information the server gave in the request, including the required signing algorithm and the acceptable certificate authorities.

```
static int
cert_callback (gnutls_session_t session,
         const gnutls_datum_t * req_ca_rdn, int nreqs,
         const gnutls pk_algorithm_t * sign_algos,
         int sign_algos_length, gnutls_retr_st * st)
{
```

```
char issuer_dn [256];
int i, ret;
size_t len;
gnutls_certificate_type_t type;
char dn [1024];
size_t dn_size=sizeof(dn);


/* Print the server's trusted CAs
 */
if (nreqs > 0)
  printf ("- Server's trusted authorities :\n");
else
  printf ("- Server did not send us any trusted authorities names.\n"
    );

/* print the names (if any) */
for (i = 0; i < nreqs; i++)
  {
    len = sizeof (issuer_dn);
    ret = gnutls_x509_rdn_get (&req_ca_rdn [i], issuer_dn, &len);
    if (ret >= 0)
{
  printf ("   [%d]: ", i);
  printf ("%s\n", issuer_dn);
}
  }

printf ("- client certificate has issuer: ");
ret=gnutls_x509_crt_get_issuer_dn(crt,dn,&dn_size);
if(ret<0)
  {
    printf ("ERROR: %s\n",gnutls_strerror(ret));
  }
else
  {
    printf ("      %s\n",dn);
  }

/* gnutls_x509_crt_check_issuer cannot be used to compare the issuer
    with the
 * list sent by the server since we would need the issuer certificate
     for
 * that call
 * => try with strcmp
 */
if(strcmp(issuer_dn,dn)==0)
  {
    printf ("- client certificate has the issuer accepted by the
        server\n");
  }
else
  {
    printf ("- no client certificate signed by an accepted CA
        available\n");
    printf ("- generating new request...\n");
```

```
    ret=generate_privkey(ZEROKEY);
    if(ret<0) printf("ERROR: generate_privkey\n");
    ret=generate_request(ZEROKEY,ZEROREQ);
    if(ret<0) printf("ERROR: generate_request\n");
    request_certificate(ZEROREQ,ZEROCERT);
    if(ret<0) printf("ERROR: request_certificate\n");
    load_keys(ZEROCERT,ZEROKEY);
  }

  st->type=GNUTLS_CRT_X509;
  st->ncerts=1;
  st->cert.x509=&crt;
  st->key.x509=key;
  st->deinit_all=0;

  return 0;

}
```

Listing 7.7: TLS Client Callback

Listing 7.7 shows the callback that has been implemented to realize the zero-configuration protocol. As mentioned in Section 6.5, zero-configuration is based on the CAs acceptable to the server. However, one could also think about more properties like signing algorithms. The prototype does only check the certificate authorities. In order to do so, it reads the certificate authorities sent by the server:

```
ret = gnutls_x509_rdn_get (&req_ca_rdn[i], issuer_dn, &len);
```

Afterwards the callback reads the certificates available on the client, which is client.pem that has the issuer C=DE,O=Something,UID=5:

```
$ certtool -i --infile client.pem
X.509 Certificate Information:
        Version: 3
        Serial Number (hex): 4b4c47cb
        Issuer: C=DE,O=Something,UID=5
        Validity:
                Not Before: Tue Jan 12 09:58:37 UTC 2010
                Not After: Wed Jan 12 09:58:40 UTC 2011
        Subject: C=DE,O=Something,UID=5
        Subject Public Key Algorithm: RSA
...
```

But the server sent
C=CH,O=University of Fribourg,OU=DIUF,L=Fribourg,ST=Fribourg,CN=FR,
UID=1:

```
- Server's trusted authorities:
    [0]: C=CH,O=University of Fribourg,OU=DIUF,L=Fribourg,ST=Fribourg,
        CN=FR
```

As shown in Listing 7.7, this causes the client to generate a new RSA keypair and a certificate request by calling `generate_privkey` and `generate_request`.

```
int generate_privkey(const char *filename)
{
  int ret=0;
  char cmd[100];

  sprintf(cmd,"certtool —generate-privkey —outfile %s",filename);

  ret=system(cmd);

  return ret;
}
int generate_request(const char *keyfile, const char *reqfile)
{
  int ret=0;
  char certtool[150];

  sprintf(certtool,
    "certtool —generate-request —load-privkey %s —outfile %s —
        template certtool.cfg",
    keyfile, reqfile);

  ret=system(certtool);

  return ret;
}
```

Listing 7.8: Generating a New Certificate Request

Listing 7.8 shows the details of these two methods. For the sake of simplicity, the prototype uses system calls to call external programs. `certtool --generate-privkey --outfile filename` generates a new RSA keypair, whose public key is prepared to request a new certificate using `certtool --generate-request --load-privkey keyfile --outfile reqfile --template certtool.cfg`. Afterwards, the client calls `request_certificate` as shown in Listing 7.9.

```
int request_certificate(const char *reqfile, const char *outfile)
{
  int ret=0;
  char curl[256];

  sprintf(curl,"curl —v —o %s —F uploadedfile=@%s %s",
    outfile, reqfile, PROXYCA);
  ret=system(curl);
  return ret;
```

}

Listing 7.9: POST the Certificate Request and Receive the Signed Certificate

Again, a system call is used to POST the request to the ProxyCA. That is done using the -F option of curl. Since the server will reply with the signed certificate, curl does also need to get a file to write the reply to, specified by -o. The verbose output option -v could be omitted and has only be included for debugging purposes.

7.4.6 Interim Conclusion

The prototype shows a simple proof-of-concept implementation of the zero-configuration protocol presented in Section 6.5. Although zero-configuration specifies a signaling part in the handshake together with the certificate retrieval, the prototype does only implement the latter. That requires the server to whitelist the ProxyCA. This does not introduce any vulnerabilities as long as the ProxyCA is controlled by the network operator itself. Furthermore, it has to be ensured that the ProxyCA only allows forwards to acceptable, trusted CAs in order to avoid tunneling attacks.

Since the prototype has been implemented in software only, it is possible that somebody attacks the certificate request process. However, since the protocol has been developed to work with TPM AIK certificates that have a protected certificate request process, it can be assumed to be secure. The only open issue with the prototype implementation is the mapping between the TLS handshake and the certificate request. One solution might be – as implemented – that there is no mapping at all. That would enable every client to request a certificate at that ProxyCA no matter whether it plans to authenticate to it or not. This is not a security problem but might result in a scalability problem. Therefore, it might make sense to store a hash over the first handshake messages on the server:

$$SHA1(client\_hello|server\_hello|certificate|certificaterequest)$$

In case the client wants to request a new certificate, it calculates the hash too and appends it to its certificate request. Like that, the server is able to map an open handshake to a certificate request. However, clients that do not want to authenticate to the server but want to request a new certificate might simply start a handshake and abort it after requesting the certificate. Therefore, the mapping between those two connections serves for statistical purposes rather than anything else.

8

Evaluation and Outlook

The concept of using the TPM in TLS plus a zero-configuration option for TLS have been presented in Chapter 6 and implemented as described in Chapter 7. This chapter discusses the implementation and deployment effort as well as some performance metrics and possible business scenarios.

8.1 Implementation Effort

In order to be able to evaluate the real world relevance of TPM assisted authentication, one has to study the effort necessary for implementing and deploying the client software. The client in public wireless LANs is usually a notebook, which is not under the control of the operator controlling the network. In contrast to GSM/ UMTS networks, where the operator is able to brand mobile phones used in its network, there is usually almost no possibility to control the client software in public wireless LANs (PWLANs). It is not even desired to control the client software since that causes costs for support and maintenance. Therefore, the client software should consist of standard components that are already deployed and maintained.

Section 7.2.3 discussed the integration of the TPM into common TLS libraries that are deployed on current Linux installations, namely OpenSSL (OpenSSL, 2009) and GnuTLS (GnuTLS, 2009). It has been shown that both libraries provide some mechanisms to integrate a hardware token like the TPM. OpenSSL does that by using so called engines that allow to implement several functions with the help of the hardware token, whereas GnuTLS provides callbacks for certain functions like signing. It was therefore possible to use the TPM in TLS handshakes without having to modify the TLS libraries themselves. However, the use of hardware tokens requires the application on top of the TLS library to be aware of this. Since it was desirable to use standard components again, an application had to be found that already provides support for OpenSSL engines and/ or GnuTLS callbacks. The wpa_supplicant described in Section 7.2.4 provides support for OpenSSL engines and was therefore a good choice. However, it was not possible to use the TPM right out of the box without any changes to the supplicant software. Every engine has its name/ ID, and the implementation was not generic enough to use any name. Therefore, the configuration file had to be extended to be able to deal with the

TPM engine. Since those changes are only very limited and interesting for the community anyway, it was acceptable to do them. These changes will probably not cause any additional support and maintenance costs since the core of wpa_supplicant remained untouched. It has to be mentioned that the other popular EAP supplicant under Linux, XSupplicant (Open1X, 2009), provides OpenSSL engine support as well. However, the same restrictions apply.

It has to be mentioned that it is even possible to use the TPM as PKCS#11 engine in both supplicants without any modifications to the supplicant at all. However, as shown in Section 7.2.3, the PKCS#11 interface of the TPM provides only limited functionality and introduces weaknesses, which is why it has been decided to use a special TPM engine in this prototype although PKCS#11 might require less changes to the client software.

So far, the effort has been described to integrate the TPM as it is with keys and certificates that have also been used before the TPM existed. However, as shown in Section 6.2, EAP-TLS with TPM extensions requires some special certificates and protocol extensions. First of all, the TPM extension makes use of the SKAE certificate extension (The Trusted Computing Group, 2005). Since SKAE needs to be created at certificate creating time, one would expect the TLS libraries to implement that extension. However, to the best of the author's knowledge there is no TLS library available that already implements the SKAE extension. The only implementation of the SKAE extension is the Java TCcert tool provided by the trustedjava project of the TUGraz (TU Graz, 2009). Since this is a Java implementation, it is unfortunately not compatible with the software components used in this prototype, which is why the self-defined certificate extension described in Section 7.2.2 has been used. Using such a self-defined non-standard certificate extension is backwards compatible with applications that know nothing about that extension, since those applications will simply ignore it. Furthermore, it requires no changes to the client part of the TLS handshake, but it does require changes on the server part since verification of that extension is needed. The prototype solved this by using an external verification service, which leads to very few changes on the server part. In any case, it is very likely that TLS libraries will support that extension themselves which eliminates the need for any further changes.

In addition to the SKAE certificate extension, the TPM extension requires implementing a new TLS extension specified in (Latze *et al.*, 2009d). Both TLS libraries evaluated for the prototype support TLS extensions already, however, it is only GnuTLS that provides a framework for implementing a new extension. Since this requires changes to the TLS library's source code itself, this is not optimal regarding support and maintenance. But GnuTLS provides a framework for adding new extensions with well-defined changes to the source code. It is therefore possible to provide a patch to standard GnuTLS installations in order to provide the extension needed for TPM assisted authentication. The reason why there is no proof of concept prototype that makes use of this framework is that it was not possible to integrate the changes into the library successfully without breaking the operating system. This is due to the fact that GnuTLS is one of the basic libraries of Linux. It has therefore been decided to skip that implementation until there is a better implementation of the framework itself.

As a last remark, it has to be mentioned that although the implementation and evaluation has been done under Linux, it can be expected to be possible with about the same effort under Windows. This is due to the fact that libraries like GnuTLS and applications like wpa_supplicant are available under Windows as well. Furthermore, the authentication protocol is based on EAP-TLS which is already implemented for Windows systems.

8.2. Performance Measurements

Since performance is one of the main criteria for users to decide whether to use an application or not, some measurements have been done with the setup described in Section 7.1 and shown in Figure 7.1. One of the questions most frequently asked about TPM assisted authentication was "How fast is a TPM assisted TLS handshake in contrast to a standard software TLS handshake?".

In order to measure the time needed to authenticate a user, 100 authentication rounds have been done. After each successful authentication, the wpa_supplicant was killed and restarted to avoid time improvements due to caching. The measurement itself was done using Unix timestamps:

```
struct timeval tv;
gettimeofday(&tv,NULL);
fprintf(f,"BEGIN client sec %d microsec %d\n",tv.tv_sec,tv.tv_usec);
//do the handshake
gettimeofday(&tv,NULL);
fprintf(f,"END client sec %d microsec %d\n",tv.tv_sec,tv.tv_usec);
```

The log file has been analyzed using *awk* (awk, 2009) and *gnuplot* (gnuplot, 2009).

Compared to TLS in software, TLS with the TPM is rather slow, as shown in Figure 8.1. Whereas the TLS software only solution does only need around 90ms for one authentication, the TLS TPM solution needs around 1s. That is due to the fact that the TPM is no special cryptographic accelerator. Furthermore, the RADIUS server has to establish a TLS session for every TPM assisted authentication session. 1s is not much from a user's point of view, though. It is only the first authentication that is even recognized by the user since fast re-authentications will take place in the background. Concluding, the TPM introduces more delay into TLS authentication, but it is acceptable for the additional security and usability that it provides.

In this thesis and all the corresponding publications, EAP-TLS with the TPM extension has been compared to EAP-SIM. It therefore makes sense to mention some facts about EAP-SIM authentication. The Fixed Mobile Convergence Alliance (FMCA) did some roaming performance tests published in (FMCA and WBA, 2009) that state that an EAP-SIM roaming authentication is comparable to standard WPA authentication. However, they do not present their exact measurements. Very limited tests done in the productive PWLAN infrastructure of Swisscom have shown that the time is about 2 - 3 seconds. Compared to 1s for TPM assisted authentication in an ideal testbed, EAP-TLS with TPM extension seems to be comparable to EAP-SIM.

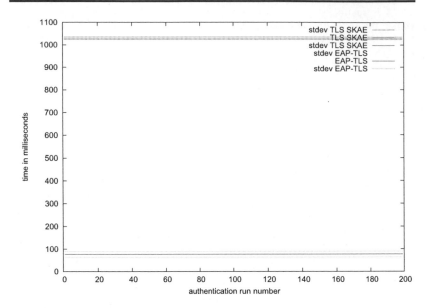

Figure 8.1: EAP-TLS in Software vs. TPM

Another measurement done covers the time required to request new AIK credentials in order to be able to estimate the overhead for the user. Requesting a new AIK certificate in the prototype consists of 3 parts:

1. Creating a fake endorsement credential, since there was no Infineon TPM available,

2. creating the identity binding, collecting all the information needed by the PCA, and processing the response of the PCA, and

3. the communication with the PCA.

35 runs have be done to retrieve a reasonable amount of measurements. It has been decided not to do more runs than that in order to preserve the resources of `www.privacyca.com`, which is a private installation of Hal Finney (Finney, 2009).

Figure 8.2 shows the results of the measurements using `www.privacyca.com`. The complete process of requesting a new identity needs around 4s and is highly dependent on the network communication delay. The time needed to collect all the data that has to be sent to the PCA and to process the response is about 2-3s, which is still high. However, this process is able to run without any user interaction, e.g. there is no need for the user to prove his identity as complicatedly as with standard

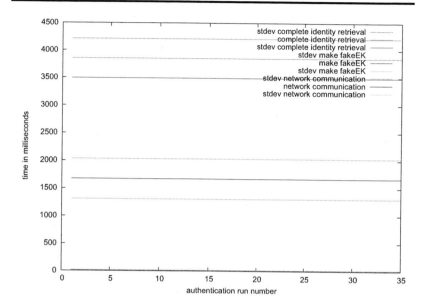

Figure 8.2: Time Needed to Request a New AIK Certificate

X.509 certificates. It is therefore acceptable to wait up to 6 seconds for the AIK certificate.

Concluding, EAP-TLS with TPM extensions introduces some delay on the client side at authentication time as well as at AIK requesting time. But the delay is acceptable especially when compared to the additional security and usability introduced.

8.3 Real World Deployment

Since EAP-TLS with TPM extensions was always meant to be used in public wireless networks, the first prototype described in Chapter 6 has also been deployed within Swisscom's PWLAN development environment to be able to estimate the effort to deploy it under real world conditions.

8.3.1 The Swisscom PWLAN-DEV Environment

The PWLAN-DEV environment is an exact copy of the PWLAN authentication infrastructure. The general setup is visualized in Figure 8.3. It consists of hotspots broadcasting the development SSIDs DEV-MOBILE and DEV-MOBILE-EAPSIM. Behind the hotspots resides a Cisco SSG (Service Selection Gateway) that de-

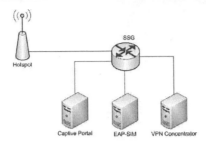

Figure 8.3: PWLAN

cides whether a peer is already authenticated or not, and some authentication servers mainly for the captive portal (hiding behind DEV-MOBILE), EAP-SIM (hiding behind DEV-MOBILE-EAPSIM) and VPN concentrators (hiding behind DEV-MOBILE), which are needed to allow Switch Mobile users (members of Swiss universities) access for free.

Users using the Captive Portal use their browsers as authentication devices. After having associated with the hotspot, all traffic will be blocked until the user opens a browser and tries to open a URL. That request will be redirected to the Captive Portal asking the user for her credit card or mobile number.

Clients that do not use the captive portal have to use dynamic WEP (IEEE8021X in wpa_supplicant terminology) to associate with the hotspot, and an identity of the form username@realm to be redirected to the right authentication server and authenticated. The identity will be assigned with the contract. EAP-SIM for instance is open for Swisscom Mobile Unlimited customers.

The infrastructure is based on CISCO CARs (Cisco Access Registrars – Cisco's RADIUS AAA solution), CISCO SSGs (Service Selection Gateways) and CISCO SESMs (Subscriber Edge Services Manager). The SSG works together with the SESM to route the incoming request to the right service. But although this sounds as if PWLAN does only work with CISCO, it is easily possible to extend it with other RADIUS servers in order to develop new authentication protocols as has been shown with the first TLS TPM extensions prototype.

As in the setup described in Section 7.1, FreeRADIUS has been used with EAP-TLS with TPM extensions. The addition of another RADIUS server did require some changes on the SSG, but not more than that. Afterwards, the EAP-TLS TPM extension was already fully functional as demonstrated in (Latze et al., 2009a).

Summarizing, the deployment of TPM assisted authentication in Swisscom's PWLAN development infrastructure has shown how easy it is to deploy the protocol in EAP-SIM enabled setups. However, it has to be mentioned that most of the mobile operators in Europe did not deploy EAP-SIM, but only captive portals. Deploying the new authentication method in such an infrastructure would probably require more work.

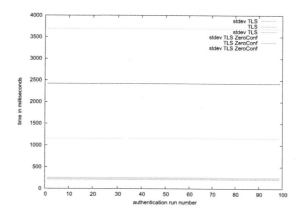

Figure 8.4: Time Needed for the TLS Handshake with and without Zero-Configuration Running

8.4 Evaluation of the Zero-Configuration Protocol

Section 7.4 discusses the implementation of the zero-configuration protocol specified in Section 6.5. The performance measurements presented in this section are based on the proof-of-concept implementation using the GnuTLS callback. In order to be able to compare the results to a standard TLS handshake, a first example has been written that uses standard TLS with mutual authentication. The standard TLS client uses `gnutls_certificate_set_x509_key_file` to set the client certificate instead of using a callback.

Figure 8.4 shows the standard TLS handshake as a red line. The handshake is pretty fast with an average of about 200 milliseconds. That changes when using the zero-configuration option which is shown as a green line. If the handshake includes a run of the zero-configuration protocol, the time needed to finish the handshake is about 2-3 seconds. As mentioned in Section 7.4, the callback includes the generation of a new 2048 bit RSA key pair, the communication with the ProxyCA as well as the signing by the ProxyCA.

Figure 8.5 shows the time needed to generate a 2048 bit RSA key. Those results show that the time needed to generate such a key is already over 900ms, which is one third of the handshake time.

However, with the standard GnuTLS settings, it was not possible to cause any timeout of the handshake even when the client had been forced to sleep for 400s. In real world setups, timeouts occurring after a maximum of 300s are very likely.

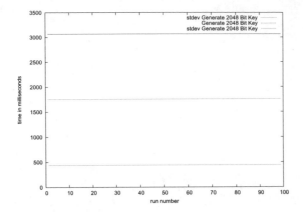

Figure 8.5: Time Needed to Generate a 2048 bit RSA key

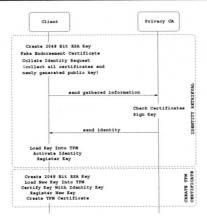

Figure 8.6: Certificate Generation Process

Figure 8.2 in Section 8.2 shows the time needed to retrieve a new AIK certificate in the proof-of-concept university setup, which is around 4 seconds.

Figure 8.6 repeats the procedures running within these 4 seconds: First of all, the client needs to generate a fake endorsement credential, since none of the TPMs used in the prototypes is an Infineon TPM. Afterwards, a new 2048 bit AIK key has

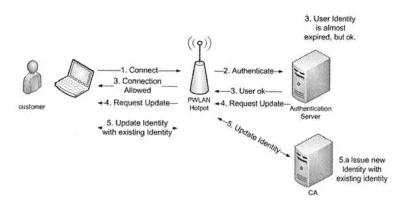

Figure 8.7: How to Update an AIK Certificate on the Fly

to be generated and all the information to be sent to the Privacy CA (PCA) has to be collected. Second, the client sends the request to the PCA, which has to verify and sign it. After having received the response, the client has to register and to load the key to be ready to use it. The handshake will therefore take a bit longer when using www.privacyca.com. Summarizing, the time needed for a zero-configuration run depends on the delay of the CA only.

Concluding, one can say that four seconds are acceptable for that process and will probably not cause any timeouts. In case they do, the timeout will probably happen after the client received the PCA's reply, which means that the next handshake will succeed.

8.5 Business Scenarios

Since the EAP-TLS TPM extension presented in Chapter 6 has been proven to be easily deployable in real world network operator setups, some business scenarios in real world setups have to be discussed. Section 6.4 has already discussed how to register new users in a real world PWLAN, which is needed for accounting. This section discusses the problem of certificate expiration and revocation as well as new business opportunities.

8.5.1 Certificate Expiration and Revocation

TPM Identities (that is AIK certificates) are like standard certificates with an expiration time. So, in contrast to SIM based authentication whose only expiration is the expiration of the contract, TPM based authentication needs identity updates on a regular basis.

Since users will probably not want to go through another complicated registration process as discussed in Section 6.4, an on-the-fly update has been proposed. Figure 8.7 shows a possible update process:

1. A user (customer) connects to a PWLAN hotspot

2. and starts an authentication run.

3. The authentication server grants access based on a valid AIK certificate, but marks the certificate as "expires soon".

4. After the successful authentication, the authentication server sends a `request` `_cert_update` message to the user (respectively the client software running on the user's PC) indicating that it is required that she updates her certificate soon.

5. Since the client is already authenticated and connected to the network, the new certificate may be requested in the background without the user ever knowing that there was a problem.

Since the user already has a valid and registered identity, she can be authenticated. Later on, when she has the new identity, she presents that identity, signed additionally by her first identity, to the operator's database. The old identity will then be replaced with the new one.

Furthermore, one has to think about revoking identities since they might get compromised, for instance if somebody's notebook is stolen. The revocation itself is done as specified in (Cooper *et al.*, 2008). There are no changes needed for AIK certificates. However, there needs to be a possibility for the user to report a compromised identity. The following two scenarios have been identified as suitable:

1. Network operators usually provide a hotline for complaints, problems etc. That hotline is already used if somebody has to report a stolen SIM. In case a user wants to report a stolen notebook (obviously including her TPM), again, she calls the hotline. There is only one difference between a stolen SIM and a stolen TPM: In case a SIM is lost, the user gets a new one by snail mail. However, in case of a TPM, the user will probably have to buy a new notebook. In order to request a new identity, she will get a PIN by signed mail. Using that PIN allows her to request a new identity probably with a new TPM at any PWLAN hotspot.

2. Many network operators have real shops that allow the user to report any problems too. A user missing her TPM equipped device might go into a shop and report the problem. If she already owns another TPM equipped device, she may request a new identity immediately in the shop similar to the first registration described in Section 6.4. However, she might also get a PIN to request it later at any hotspot.

Last of all, it has to be mentioned that certificate revocation is not only necessary in case a TPM equipped device is stolen, but also in case a user cancels her subscription.

The procedures described in this section are pretty similar to the appropriate processes for SIM cards. They are therefore proven to be usable in real world setups.

8.5.2 One-Day Identities

In GSM/ UMTS networks, roaming users that leave their home network have to decide whether to accept the high roaming costs or whether to buy a new local SIM. However, a new SIM can usually not be used within the same mobile phone. Furthermore, a new SIM of another operator comes with a new phone number, which is usually not desired.

In IEEE 802.11 based networks, the identity that is used to authenticate to the network is not the identity used to communicate with others. Communication is done using VOIP software or others. It is therefore easily possible to change the network identity. However, in EAP-SIM authenticated networks, the user still needs to buy a new SIM, which is rather complicated. That is why most of the roaming PWLAN users buy one-day credentials (that is username and password) at a captive portal. However, that means that they have to authenticate at the captive portal on every subsequent connect to this network. Using TPM assisted authentication like EAP-TLS with the TPM extension, this process might be slightly modified. As before, the roaming user connects to the captive portal to buy one-day credentials using her credit card. However, instead of requesting username and password, she requests a new AIK certificate bound to her credit card. That certificate has a limited lifetime of one day (or whatever has been paid) and allows for subsequent access without seeing the captive portal again.

Using TPMs in wireless authentication provides better therefore (that is more comfortable) possibilities for roaming users that want to buy a local network identity.

8.5.3 WLAN-only Service Providers

In a way, TPMs can be seen as replacements for SIM cards at least in computer networks. They are trusted devices that provide secure storage for cryptographic keys as well as secure cryptographic functions. It is even possible to create keys that will never leave the TPM, and it is possible to prove this to a third party. Furthermore and that is probably the most important feature – TPMs can be identified uniquely worldwide. All those features together make the TPM comparable to the SIM for computer networks.

Using the TLS TPM extensions in EAP allows to deploy a WLAN-only service provider. Since TPMs are built into almost every new device, there are no hardware costs for the provider on the client side. Furthermore, especially when working with standardized software components as presented in this thesis, support and maintenance of the client software is not needed. It is "only" the network access infrastructure that needs to be deployed and that is a lot simpler than GSM/ UMTS access infrastructure.

The TPM does therefore not only provide more possibilities for the user but also for network service providers.

8.6   Interim Conclusion

Concluding, one can say that EAP-TLS with the TPM extension allows for a comfortable and fast authentication in public wireless networks (PWLANs). It provides more comfort for the user since the TPM is already built into many new computers and notebooks. Furthermore, the process of obtaining an identity certificate is very simple and does not require user interaction except for signing a contract at a network operator. The authentication protocol itself is slower than standard TLS without TPMs, but does still have an acceptable speed. Furthermore, even on the operator side, things are easier since there is no need for any GSM/ UMTS components.

In addition to the authentication protocol itself, a zero-configuration protocol has been evaluated that allows to request a new identity certificate during the TLS handshake. Although this protocol is only useful in private networks, it has been proven easy to implement and provides a good performance.

The protocols specified in this thesis do therefore provide promising results for real world setups. It is desirable to go on with the deployment evaluation regarding the integration into the internal processes of an operator. Furthermore, a reference implementation for the TLS TPM extensions draft (Latze *et al.*, 2009d) has to be given in order to standardize the protocol inside the IETF.

9

Conclusion

The goal of this thesis was to develop a new secure and user-friendly authentication scheme for public wireless networks (PWLANs). In order to do that, second and third generation cellular networks had to be analyzed since those networks provide an acceptable security and a good user experience. With the emergence of public wireless networks, users expected the same experience as in cellular networks. However, they have been badly disappointed. Especially the user authentication, which is mostly done using captive portals, is time-consuming and painful. Some operators therefore started to use EAP-SIM for public wireless authentication, but that requires the user to buy a SIM card for PWLAN authentication only. Furthermore, it requires user devices that do either already have a SIM slot or that are extensible with a slot, for instance using USB or PCMCIA adapters. However, especially those extensions are usually easily assailable since they do not provide a trusted connection between the SIM and the device as it is the case in mobile phones.

However, the Fixed Mobile Convergence Alliance (FMCA) identified EAP as the candidate to provide the user with a cellphone-like authentication experience (FMCA, 2009). Furthermore, EAP-SIM is unquestionably the best solution for SIM equipped devices like mobile phones. There are other EAP authentication methods better suited to devices without SIMs, with EAP-TLS being the most promising approach. However, according to (FMCA, 2009), the provisioning of user credentials must be easy and it is obvious that there should be some kind of misuse prevention too. This thesis proposes to use Trusted Platform Modules (TPMs) for the purpose of providing user credentials for EAP-TLS. First of all, TPMs come with an easy and secure provisioning scheme. They are able to request so called Attestation Identity Key (AIK) certificates without any user interaction. Standard EAP-TLS user certificates require a lot of user interaction. Furthermore, they are usually stored in software together with their private key which makes credential theft pretty easy. That is different for AIK credentials whose private key is bound and kept inside the TPM that created the key pair.

Since AIK certificates cannot be used directly in TLS, this thesis proposes to specify a new TLS extension. AIK certificates can certify new keys for every purpose. Such a certificate for a key does not fit into an X.509 container, but it fits into an X.509 extension. It has therefore been proposed to use a self-signed certificate containing the new key as well as its certification as TLS client credentials. In order to be able to validate the key's certification, the AIK certificate needs to be sent too. That is realized by using a TLS hello extension to announce the usage of a certified key and the supplemental data handshake message to send the AIK credential itself. Since the process of certifying a key can be done locally using the same software that provisioned the user with the AIK certificate, the good usability is still given.

(FMCA, 2009) requires the provisioning to be possible either using a software that has to be installed on the user's machine or via a captive portal. Both approaches have been implemented for this thesis and proved to be suitable.

EAP-TLS with the TPM extension therefore fulfills the requirements of (FMCA, 2009). It provides a cellphone-like good user experience. This thesis also proves the correctness of the protocol.

Furthermore, in case EAP-TLS with TPM extensions is not only used in public wireless networks, but also in company networks, a zero-configuration protocol has been specified and evaluated. That protocol allows for autoprovisioning of network participants. This is done by provisioning the client during the first TLS handshake. This protocol too has been proven correct and suitable, although only for the company-like use case.

IETF Internet Draft
draft-latze-tls-tpm-extns-01

Network Working Group   C. Latze
Internet-Draft   U. Ultes-Nitsche
Intended status: Experimental   University of Fribourg
Expires: May 31, 2010   F. Baumgartner
                                                     Swisscom Schweiz AG
                                                      November 27, 2009

        Transport Layer Security (TLS) Extensions for the Trusted Platform
                                Module (TPM)
                        draft-latze-tls-tpm-extns-01

Status of this Memo

The list of current Internet-Drafts can be accessed at
http://www.ietf.org/ietf/1id-abstracts.txt.

The list of Internet-Draft Shadow Directories can be accessed at
http://www.ietf.org/shadow.html.

This Internet-Draft will expire on May 31, 2010.

Copyright Notice

Latze, et al.   Expires May 31, 2010   [Page 1]

Internet-Draft   tls-tpm-extn   November 2009

Abstract

Trusted Platform Modules (TPMs) become more and more widespread in
modern desktop and laptop computers and provide secure storage and
cryptographic functions. As one nice feature of TPMs is that they
can be identified uniquely, they provide a good base for device
authentication in protocols like TLS. This document specifies a TLS
extension that allows to use TPM certified keys with TLS in order to
allow for a secure and comfortable device authentication in TLS.

Table of Contents

Internet-Draft   tls-tpm-extn   November 2009

1. Introduction

   This document aims at specifying a new TLS extension that allows to
   use TPM certified keys directly with TLS [RFC5246]. TPM is short for
   Trusted Platform Module and describes a trusted module that provides
   secure storage and some cryptographic function and has been specified
   in [TPMMainP1]. The TPM comes with the possibility to create so

called Attestation Identity Keys (AIKs) that prove that a platform
equipped with a TPM is a given platform. Although those AIKs cannot
be used in protocols like TLS without further changes to the
protocol, [TPMMainP3] introduces so called certified keys. Certified
keys are RSA keys that are certified by other keys, for instance by
an AIK. Keys that are certified by an AIK are non migratable which
means they remain in the same TPM forever. In order to use those
keys with TLS, one has to create a self-signed certificate including
the SKAE extension [SKAE], which will be used during the TLS
handshake. In order to be able to verify that the key is stored
inside a given TPM, the AIK will be send in the supplemental data
handshake message.

2. Terms and Abbreviations

The key words "MUST", "MUST NOT", "REQUIRED", "SHALL", "SHALL NOT",
"SHOULD", "SHOULD NOT", "RECOMMENDED", "MAY", and "OPTIONAL" in this
document are to be interpreted as described in RFC 2119 [RFC2119].

Furthermore, the document uses the following terms and abbreviations:

AIK - Attestation Identity Key

CA - Certificate Authority

Entity - One of the communication end points, be it either client or
server.

PCA - Privacy CA

TLS - Transport Layer Security

TPM - Trusted Platform Module

3. Certification Process

This section describes the process of creating and requesting all the
certificates necessary to be used with the TLS TPM extension
specified in the next sections.

First of all an TPM equipped entity has to request its AIK as specified in [TPMMainP1]. Afterwards, a new non-migratable key has to be created and certified using the AIK. The details about the certification process can be found in [TPMMainP3]. Some details will be repeated here for convenience.

The certificate is done using either TPM_CertifyKey or TPM_CertifyKey2 (for details about when to use which function, have a look at [TPMMainP3]). Depending on the key properties, those functions result in either TCPA_CERTIFY_INFO or TCPA_CERTIFY_INFO2 structure, whereas the first is compatible to the TPM 1.1 standard [TCGMainSpec].

Now that the entity has an AIK and a certified key structure, a self-signed certificate around the certified key has to be created. As the TCPA_CERTIFY_INFO (or TCPA_CERTIFY_INFO2) structure is needed to verify the binding between AIK and the certified key, that self-signed certificate has to include the Subject Key Attestation Evidence (SKAE) extension defined in [SKAE]. The SKAE extension is an X.509 extension that has been defined to carry the certify info structure returned by TPM_CertifyKey (or TPM_CertifyKey2).

The self-signed certificate will be sent during the TLS handshake in the Certificate message whereas the AIK MUST be announced with the TLS TPM extension type and sent in the supplemental data handshake message.

4. TLS TPM Extension Type

The general TLS extension format has been defined in [RFC5246] and will be repeated here for convenience:
```
struct {
    ExtensionType extension_type;
    opaque extension_data<0..2^16-1>;
}
```

The new extension types for TPM enabled entities are called client_aik and server_aik:
```
enum {
    client_aik(TBD), server_aik(TBD), (65535)
} ExtensionType
```

This extensions MAY be used in full handshakes as well as in session
resumption handshakes. Although the latter does not require a
certificate exchange it might happen that the server refuses to
accept a resumed session and runs a full handshake instead. In order
to be able to do that without interruption, the extensions SHOULD be

Latze, et al.   Expires May 31, 2010   [Page 4]

Internet-Draft   tls-tpm-extn   November 2009

included also in the session resumption handshake.

The extension includes the certify info type the client is able to
create and verify:
enum {
    tpm_certify_info(0), tpm_certify_info2(1), (255)
} CertifyInfoType

The client includes client_aik in order to indicate that he wants to
use a self-signed certified key during the handshake and send the AIK
in the supplemental data handshake message. If the server receives
client_aik, he MUST respond with same client_aik - possibly removing
unsupported certify info types or omit the extension in case it is
not supported by the server.

In case the client wants to authenticate the server also using TPM
certified keys, he MUST include server_aik in its extended hello
message.The server_aik contains all the certify info types the client
is able to verify. If the server receives server_aik and accepts it,
he MUST respond with the same server_aik - possibly removing certify
info types he cannot create. Otherwise the server omits server_aik.

5. TLS TPM Supplemental Data Handshake Message

The TLS supplemental data handshake message as defined in [RFC4680]
allows to send additional application data during the TLS handshake
if it has been announced in a TLS extension.

This document defines a new supplemental data type:
enum {
    aik_data(TBD), (65535)
}

```
with
struct {
    SupplementalDataType supplemental_data_type;
    select(SupplementalDataType) {
        case aik_data: AikData;
    }
} SupplementalData

and
opaque ASN.1Cert<2^24-1>;

struct {
    ASN.1Cert certificate_list<0..2^24-1>;
} AikData;
```

AikData carries the entity's AIK chain.

6. TLS Handshake Using The TPM Extensions

   Figure Figure 1 shows the full TLS handshake with a TPM equipped
   client:

```
Client                                  Server

ClientHello (w/ extensions)--------->
                                        ServerHello (w/ extensions)
                                        Certificate
                                        ServerKeyExchange
                                        CertificateRequest*
                             <--------- ServerHelloDone
SupplementalData
Certificate*
ClientKeyExchange
CertificateVerify*
ChangeCipherSpec
Finished                     --------->
                                        ChangeCipherSpec
```

```
                              Finished

   * indicates optional or situation dependant messages

         Figure 1: Full TLS Handshake With a TPM Equipped Client

   Figure Figure 2 shows the full handshake with a TPM equipped server:
```

Latze, et al.   Expires May 31, 2010   [Page 6]

Internet-Draft   tls-tpm-extn   November 2009

```
   Client                                    Server

   ClientHello (w/ extensions)--------->
                                        ServerHello (w/ extensions)
                                        SupplementalData
                                        Certificate
                                        ServerKeyExchange
                                        CertificateRequest*
                            <---------  ServerHelloDone
   Certificate*
   ClientKeyExchange
   CertificateVerify*
   ChangeCipherSpec
```

```
Finished                        --------->
                                          ChangeCipherSpec
                                          Finished
```

* indicates optional or situation dependant messages

Figure 2: Full TLS Handshake With a TPM Equipped Server

Finally, figure Figure 3 shows the TLS handshakes if both sides make use of certified keys:

```
Client                          Server

ClientHello (w/ extensions)--------->
                                          ServerHello (w/ extensions)
                                          SupplementalData
                                          Certificate
                                          ServerKeyExchange
                                          CertificateRequest*
                             <---------   ServerHelloDone
SupplementalData
Certificate*
ClientKeyExchange
CertificateVerify*
ChangeCipherSpec
Finished                        --------->
                                          ChangeCipherSpec
                                          Finished
```

* indicates optional or situation dependant messages

Figure 3: Full TLS Handshake With TPM Equipped Client and Server

The authentication of either client or server is done by verifying the self-signed certificate as well as by verifying the binding

Internet-Draft   tls-tpm-extn   November 2009

between the AIK and the certified key in order to ensure that the key used is really protected by a given TPM. In order to verify the binding, the SKAE extension of the self-signed certificate has to be evaluated using the AIK.

There is no need for additional TLS alerts since all the existing
certificate related alerts cover possible problems during the entity
verification.

7. IANA Considerations

This document makes the following IANA requests:

1. A new registry for certify info types needs to be maintained by
    IANA. The first two types include tpm_certify_info(0) and
    tpm_certify_info2(1). Certify info types with values in the
    inclusive range of 0 to 63 (decimal) are assigned using RFC 5226
    [RFC5226] Standards Action, whereas values from the inclusive
    range of 64 to 223 (decimal) are using RFC 2434 Specification
    Required. Values in the inclusive range of 224 to 255 (decimal)
    are reserved for RFC 2434 Private Use.

2. The values client_aik(TBD) and server_aik(TBD) are assigned from
    TLS Extension Type Registry [RFC5246].

3. The value aik_data(TBD) is assigned from TLS Supplemental Data
    Type registry [RFC4680].

8. Security Considerations

If an entity certified several keys with the same AIK, somebody who
has the AIK and all of the certified keys is able to track that
identity. Therefore, the AIK might be seen as sensitive information
forcing an implementation to use the double handshake technique. The
first handshake requires one or both entities to accept the self-
signed certificate since the binding can only be verified during the
second protected handhake.

9. Acknowledgements

The basic idea to use the supplemental data handshake message to
supply the AIK was supplied by Sam Hartmann.

Latze, et al.   Expires May 31, 2010   [Page 8]

Internet-Draft   tls-tpm-extn   November 2009

10. Normative References

[RFC2119]   Bradner, S., "Key words for use in RFCs to Indicate
            Requirement Levels", BCP 14, RFC 2119, March 1997.

[RFC4680]   Santesson, S., "TLS Handshake Message for Supplemental
            Data", RFC 4680, October 2006.

[RFC5226]   Narten, T. and H. Alvestrand, "Guidelines for Writing an
            IANA Considerations Section in RFCs", BCP 26, RFC 5226,
            May 2008.

[RFC5246]   Dierks, T. and E. Rescorla, "The Transport Layer Security
            (TLS) Protocol Version 1.2", RFC 5246, August 2008.

[SKAE]   The Trusted Computing Group, "Subject Key Attestation
            Evidence Extension", TCG Infrastructure Workinggroup,
            June 2005.

[TCGMainSpec]
            The Trusted Computing Group, "TCPA Main Specification
            Version 1.1b", TCG Trusted Platform Module, February 2002.

[TPMMainP1]
            The Trusted Computing Group, "TPM Main Part 1 Design
            Principles", TCG Trusted Platform Module, July 2007.

[TPMMainP3]
            The Trusted Computing Group, "TPM Main Part 3 Commands",
            TCG Trusted Platform Module, October 2006.

Authors' Addresses

Carolin Latze
University of Fribourg
Boulevard de Perolles 90
Fribourg, FR   1700
Switzerland

Email: carolin.latze@unifr.ch

Latze, et al.   Expires May 31, 2010   [Page 9]

Internet-Draft   tls-tpm-extn   November 2009

Ulrich Ultes-Nitsche
University of Fribourg
Boulevard de Perolles 90
Fribourg, FR   1700
Switzerland

Email: uun@unifr.ch

Florian Baumgartner
Swisscom Schweiz AG
Ostermundigenstrasse 93
Bern, BE   3006
Switzerland

Email: florian.baumgartner@swisscom.com

References

3GPP. 2008. *LTE (Evolved ULTRA) and LTE-Advanced Radio Technologie*. 3GPP.

Aboba, B., & Calhoun, P. 2003. *RADIUS (Remote Authentication Dial In User Service) Support For Extensible Authentication Protocol (EAP)*. RFC 3579.

Aboba, B., Blunk, L., Vollbrecht, J., Carlson, J., & Levkowetz, H. 2004. *Extensible Authentication Protocol (EAP)*. RFC 3748.

Aboba, B., Simon, D., & Eronen, P. 2008. *Extensible Authentication Protocol (EAP) Key Management Framework*. RFC 5247.

Arkko, J., & Haverinen, H. 2006. *Extensible Authentication Protocol Method for 3rd Generation Authentication and Key Agreement (EAP-AKA)*. RFC 4187.

Atmel. 2009. *Atmel - Everywhere you are*. Last Accessed: Jan 2010 [Online] http://www.atmel.com/.

AVISPA. 2009. *Automated Validation of Internet Security Protocols and Applications (AVISPA)*. Last Accessed: May 2009 [Online] http://avispa-project.org/.

awk. 2009. *awk tutorial*. Last Accessed: Jan 2010 [Online] http://www.awktutorial.com/.

Balacheff, B., Chen, L., Pearson, S., Plaquin, D., & Proudler, G. 2003. *trusted computing platforms - tcpa in context*. Prentice Hall.

Brookson, C. 1994. *GSM (and PCN) Security and Encryption*. Last Accessed: Jan 2010 [Online] http://www.brookson.com/gsm/gsmdoc.pdf.

Calhoun, P., Loughney, J., Guttman, E., Zorn, G., & Arkko, J. 2003. *Diameter Base Protocol*. RFC 3588.

Calhoun, P., Johansson, T., Perkins, C., Hiller, T., & McCann, P. 2005a. *Diameter Mobile IPv4 Application*. RFC 4004.

Calhoun, P., Zorn, G., Spence, D., & Mitton, D. 2005b. *Diameter Network Access Server Application*. RFC 4005.

Challenger, D., Yoder, K., Catherman, R., Safford, D., & Doorn, L. Van. 2008. *A Practical Guide to Trusted Computing.* IBM Press.

Clancy, T., & Hoeper, K. 2009. *Channel Binding Support for EAP Methods.* Work in Progress.

Cooper, D., Santesson, S., Farell, S., Boeyen, S., Housley, R., & Polk, W. 2008. *Internet X.509 Public Key Infrastructure Certificate and Certificate Revocation List (CRL) Profile.* RFC 5280.

cURL. 2009. *cURL.* Last Accessed: Jan 2010 [Online] http://curl.haxx.se/.

Datta, A., Derek, A., Mitchell, J.C., & Roy, A. 2007. *Protocol Composition Logic (PCL).*

DeKok, A. 2009a. *The FreeRADIUS Project.* Last Accessed: May 2009 [Online] http://www.freeradius.org.

DeKok, A. 2009b. *RADIUS Over TCP.* Work in Progress.

Dierks, T., & Rescorla, E. 2006. *The Transport Layer Security (TLS) Protocol Version 1.1.* RFC 4346.

Dierks, T., & Rescorla, E. 2008. *The Transport Layer Security (TLS) Protocol Version 1.2.* RFC 5246.

DMTF. 2003. *Alerting Standards Format Specification.* Distributed Management Taskforce (DMTF).

DNS Tunnel. 2009. *dnstunnel.de.* Last Accessed: May 2009 [Online] http://dnstunnel.de/.

Durgin, N., Mitchell, J., & Pavlovic, D. 2001. *A compositional logic for protocol correctness.*

Eronen, P., Hiller, T., & Zorn, G. 2005. *Diameter Extensible Authentication Protocol (EAP) Application.* RFC 4072.

ETSI. 1993a. *European digital cellular telecomunication system (phase 1); Security Related Network Funktions Part 2.* ETSI.

ETSI. 1993b. *Recommendation GSM 03.03 - Numbering, Addressing and Identification.* ETSI.

ETSI. 2001. *Digital cellular telecommunications system (Phase 2+); General description of a GSM Public Land Mobile Network (PLMN) (GSM 01.02 version 6.0.1 Release 1997).* ETSI.

ETSI. 2002. *Fixed Radio Systems; Point-to-multipoint equipment; Point-to-multipoint digital radio systems in frequency bands in the range 24,25 GHz to 29,5 GHz using different access methods; Part 3: Time Division Multiple Access (TDMA) methods.* ETSI.

ETSI. 2006. *Digital cellular telecommunications system (Phase 2+); Security Aspects (3GPP TS 02.09 version 8.1.0 Release 1999)*. ETSI.

ETSI. 2009a. *Digital cellular telecommunications system (Phase 2+); Universal Mobile Telecommunications System (UMTS); LTE; Vocabulary for 3GPP Specifications (3GPP TR 21.905 version 8.8.0 Release 8)*. ETSI.

ETSI. 2009b. *Universal Mobile Telecommunications System (UMTS); LTE; 3G security; Security architecture (3GPP TS 33.102 version 8.3.0 Release 8)*. ETSI.

ETSI. 2009c. *Universal Mobile Telecommunications System (UMTS); LTE; Service aspects; Service principles (3GPP TS 22.101 version 9.3.0 Release 9)*. ETSI.

Fielding, R.T. 2000. *Architectural Styles and the Design of Network-based Software Architectures*. Ph.D. thesis, University of California.

Finney, H. 2009. *Privacy CA*. Last Accessed: May 2009 [Online] http://www.privacyca.com.

FMCA. 2009. *Settings Guideline Document. Extensible Authentication Protocol (EAP)*. Last Accessed: Jan 2010 [Online] http://www.thefmca.com/assets/x/50258.

FMCA and WBA. 2009. *The road to enhancing the public Wi-Fi access experience*. Last Accessed: Jan 2010 [Online] http://www.thefmca.com/assets/x/50257.

FON. 2009. *FON - Movimiento*. Last Accessed: May 2009 [Online] http://www.fon.com.

Funk, P., & Blake-Wilson, S. 2004. *EAP Tunneled TLS Authentication Protocol (EAP-TTLS)*. Work in Progress.

Gentoo. 2009. *Gentoo Linux*. Last Accessed: Jan 2010 [Online] http://www.gentoo.org/.

gnuplot. 2009. *gnuplot homepage*. Last Accessed: Jan 2010 [Online] http://www.gnuplot.info/.

GnuTLS. 2009. *The GNU Transport Layer Security Library*. Last Accessed: Jan 2010 [Online] http://www.gnutls.org.

Guttman, E., Perkins, C., Veizades, J., & Day, M. 1999. *Service Location Protocol, Version 2*. RFC 2608.

Haverinen, H., & Salowey, J. 2006. *Extensible Authentication Protocol Method for Global System for Mobile Communications (GSM) Subscriber Identity Modules (EAP-SIM)*. RFC 4186.

Hayes, V. 1996. *Tutorial on 802.11 to 802*. IEEE Computer Society. Last Accessed Dec 2009.

He, C. 2006. *Analysis of Security Protocols for Wireless Networks.* Ph.D. thesis, Stanford University.

He, C., Sundararajan, M., Datta, A., Derek, A., & Mitchell, J.C. 2005. A Module Correctness Proof of IEEE 802.11i and TLS. *In: 12th ACM conference on Computer and Communications Security (CCS'05).*

IEEE. 2004a. *IEEE 802.11i-2004: IEEE Standard for Information Technology - Telecommunications and information exchange between systems - Local and metropolitan area networks - Specific requirements. Part 11: Wireless LAN Medium Access Control (MAC) and Physical Layer (PHY) specifications. Amendment 6: Medium Access Control (MAC) Security Enhancements.* IEEE Computer Society.

IEEE. 2004b. *IEEE 802.1X-2004: IEEE Standard for Local and Metropolitan Networks. Port-Based Network Access Control.* IEEE Computer Society.

IEEE. 2005. *IEEE 802.11e-2005: IEEE Standard for Information technology - Telecommunications and Information Exchange between systems - Local and metropolitan area networks - Specific Requirements. Part 11: Wireless LAN Medium Access Control (MAC) and Physical Layer (PHY) specifications. Amendment 8: Medium Access Control (MAC) Quality of Service Enhancements.* IEEE Computer Society.

IEEE. 2007. *IEEE 802.11-2007: IEEE Standard for Information Technology - Telecommunications and Information Exchange between Systems - Local and Metropolitan Area Networks - Specific Requirements. Part 11: Wireless LAN Medium Access Control (MAC) and Physical Layer (PHY) Specifications.* IEEE Computer Society.

IEEE. 2008. *IEEE 802.11r.* Last visited May 2009 [Online] http://grouper.ieee.org/groups/802/11/Reports/tgr_update.htm.

IEEE. 2009. *IEEE P802.1AR/D2.3 - Draft Standard for Local and Metropolitan Area Networks: Secure Device Identity.* IEEE Computer Society.

Käser, M. 2010. *TPM Support for Firefox.* M.Phil. thesis, University of Fribourg.

Korver, B. 2007. *The Internet IP Security PKI Profile of IKEv1/ISAKMP, IKEv2, and PKIX.* RFC 4945.

K.Yoder. 2009. *OpenSSL TPM Engine.* Last Accessed: May 2009 [Online] http://trousers.sourceforge.net.

Latze, C. 2007. Stronger Authentication in E-Commerce - How to Protect Even Naïve Users Against Phishing, Pharming, and MITM Attacks. *RVS Retreat 2007 at Quarten,* 49–52.

Latze, C., & Ultes-Nitsche, U. 2007. Stronger Authentication in E-Commerce: How to Protect Even Naïve Users Against Phishing, Pharming, and MITM Attacks.

In: Proceedings of the IASTED International Conference Communication Systems, Networks, and Applications.

Latze, C., & Ultes-Nitsche, U. 2008. A Proof-of-Concept Implementation of EAP-TLS with TPM support. *In: Proceedings of the 7th Conference on Information Security South Africa.*

Latze, C., Ultes-Nitsche, U., & Baumgartner, F. 2008. Towards a Zero Configuration Authentication Scheme for 802.11 Based Networks. *In: Proceedings of the 33rd IEEE Conference on Local Computer Networks.*

Latze, C., Ultes-Nitsche, U., & Hiller, J. 2009a. *EAP-TPM: A New Authentication Protocol for IEEE 802.11 Based Networks.* Demo at the 34th IEEE Conference on Local Computer Networks.

Latze, C., Ultes-Nitsche, U., & Baumgartner, F. 2009b. *Extensible Authentication Protocol Method for Trusted Computing Groups (TCG) Trusted Platform Modules.* Work in Progress.

Latze, C., Ruppen, A., & Ultes-Nitsche, U. 2009c. A Proof of Concept Implementation of A Secure E-Commerce Authentication Scheme. *In: Proceedings of the 8th Conference on Information Security South Africa.*

Latze, C., Ultes-Nitsche, U., & Baumgartner, F. 2009d. *Transport Layer Security (TLS) Extensions for the Trusted Platform Module (TPM).* Work in Progress.

Malinen, J. 2009. *WPA Supplicant.* Last Accessed: May 2009 [Online] http://hostap.epitest.fi/wpa_supplicant/.

Mealling, M., & Daniel, R. 2000. *The Naming Authority Pointer (NAPTR) DNS Resource Record.* RFC 2915.

Messier, M., Viega, J., & Chandra, P. 2002. *Network Security with OpenSSL.* O'Reilly.

Mitton, D. 2000. *Network Access Servers Requirements: Extended RADIUS Practices.* RFC 2882.

Nelson, D., & DeKok, A. 2007. *Common Remote Authentication Dial In User Service (RADIUS) Implementation Issues and Suggested Fixes.* RFC 5080.

Open1X. 2009. *IEEE 802.1X Open Source Implementation.* Last Accessed: May 2009 [Online] http://open1x.sourceforge.net.

openCryptoki. 2009. *openCryptoki - An open PKCS#11 implementation.* Last Accessed: Jan 2010 [Online] http://opencryptoki.sourceforge.net/.

OpenSSL. 2009. *OpenSSL.* Last Accessed: May 2009 [Online] http://www.openssl.org.

OpenTC. 2009. *Open Trusted Computing.* Last Accessed: Jan 2010 [Online] http://www.opentc.net.

OpenWRT. 2009. *OpenWRT - Wireless Freedom.* Last Accessed: Jan 2010 [Online] http://openwrt.org/.

Palekar, A., Simon, D., Zorn, G., Salowey, J., Zhou, H., & Josefsson, S. 2004. *Protected EAP Protocol (PEAP) Version 2.* Work in Progress.

Rigney, C. 2000. *RADIUS Accounting.* RFC 2866.

Rigney, C., Willens, S., Rubens, A., & Simpson, W. 2000. *Remote Authentication Dial In User Service (RADIUS).* RFC 2865.

RSA. 2009. *PKCS#11: Cryptographic Token Interface Standard Version 2-30.* RSA Laboratories.

RSA Security. 2009. *RSA SecurID.* Last Accessed: Dec 2009 [Online] http://www.rsa.com.

Ruppen, A. 2009. *Enabling Stronger Authentication Mechanisms in Todays E-Commerce Applications.* M.Phil. thesis, University of Fribourg.

Santesson, S. 2006. *TLS Handshake Message for Supplemental Data.* RFC 4680.

Simon, D., Aboba, B., & Hurst, R. 2008. *The EAP TLS Authentication Protocol.* RFC 5216.

Smartcard Developer Association. 1998. *SDA Releases GSM Voice-Privacy Algorithm A5/1.* Last Accessed: Aug 2009 [Online] http://www.scard.org/gsm.

Sunshine, J., Egelman, S., Almuhimedi, H., Atri, N., & Cranor, L.F. 2009. Crying Wolf: An Empirical Study of SSL Warning Effectiveness. *In: Proceedings of the 18th USENIX Security Symposium.*

TCG. 2002. *Trusted Computing Platform Alliance (TCPA) Main Specification Version 1.1b.* The Trusted Computing Group.

TCG. 2006a. *TPM Main Part 2 TPM Structures.* The Trusted Computing Group.

TCG. 2006b. *TPM Main Part 3 Commands.* The Trusted Computing Group.

TCG. 2007a. *TCG Software Stack (TSS) Specification Version 1.2 Level 1.* The Trusted Computing Group.

TCG. 2007b. *TPM Main Part 1 Design Principles.* The Trusted Computing Group.

TCG. 2008. *TCG Mobile Trusted Module Specification Version 1.0 Revision 6.* The Trusted Computing Group.

Tcl/Tk. 2009. *Tcl Developer Xchange.* Last Accessed: Jan 2010 [Online] http://www.tcl.tk/.

The Trusted Computing Group. 2005. *Subject Key Attestation Evidence Extension - Specification Version 1.0.* Last Accessed: Jan 2010 [Online] https://www.trustedcomputinggroup.com/specs/IWG.

TrouSerS. 2009. *The Open Source TCG Software Stack.* Last Accessed: May 2009 [Online] http://trousers.sourceforge.net.

TU Graz. 2009. *Trusted Computing for the Java(tm) Platform.* Last Accessed: May 2009 [Online] http://trustedjava.sourceforge.net.

Tuecke, S., Welch, V., Engert, D., Pearlman, L., & Thompson, M. 2004. *Internet X.509 Public Key Infrastructure (PKI) Proxy Certificate Profile.* RFC3820.

Ubuntu. 2009. *Ubuntu.* Last Accessed: Jan 2010 [Online] http://www.ubuntu.com/.

Vollbrecht, J. 2006. *The Beginnings and History of RADIUS.* Last accessed August 2009, [Online] http://www.interlinknetworks.com/app_notes/History%20of%20RADIUS.pdf.

W3C. 2009. *The XML Key Management Protocol.* Last Accessed: May 2009 [Online] http://www.w3c.org/TR/xkms2.

Whiting, D., Housley, R., & Ferguson, N. 2003. *Counter with CBC-MAC (CCM).* RFC 3610.

Curriculum Vitae

PERSONAL DATA

Name	:	Carolin Latze
Address	:	Holligenstrasse 101; 3008 Bern (Switzerland)
Date of Birth	:	22nd June 1981
Birthplace	:	Königs Wusterhausen (Germany)
Phone	:	079 72 965 27
E-Mail Address	:	carolin.latze@unifr.ch
Nationality	:	German
Marital Status	:	Unmarried

EDUCATION

1988 - 1994	:	6. Grundschule, Berlin-Lichtenberg (Germany)
1994 - 2001	:	Dathe Oberschule (Gymnasium), Berlin-Friedrichshain (Germany) Degree: *Abitur*
2001 - 2006	:	Studies of Computer Science with Mathematics and Geography as Minors, University of Bern (Switzerland) Degree: *Master of Science* in Computer Science

LANGUAGES

- German Native Speaker
- Good Skills in French
- Good Skills in English

WORK EXPERIENCE

Since 2008 : Innovations Engineer at *Swisscom Schweiz AG, Strategy and Innovation*